SPAIN
SPANISH with PHRASES

Heather and John Leigh
and Salvador Ortiz-Carboneres

Illustrated by Joseph McEwan

Designed by Graham Round
Edited by Jane Chisholm

The material in this book is also published as two
separate Usborne books with the titles:
Junior Guide to Spain and *Junior Guide to Spanish.*

Part 1. Guide to Spain

First published in 1980 by
Usborne Publishing Ltd,
20 Garrick Street, London WC2E 9BJ,
England.

Printed in Belgium by
Henri Proost, Turnhout.

How to use this part of the Book

This is a picture guide filled with useful and interesting information about Spain. Take it on holiday with you, and find out about exciting things to see and do, or read it at home to find out what it is like in Spain.

The book explains some of the new and unusual things you will see. It describes what to eat and where to go, and suggests some fun things to do, such as visiting a film set where Westerns are made, watching fiestas, or playing chess with giant pieces. It makes visits to castles and churches fun by giving you things to look out for. You can find out all about shops and money, and it tells you about Spanish beaches too.

There are lots of interesting things to spot, which will make your travelling fun. When you see something, put a tick in the square next to the picture. The words in heavy type, like **this**, tell you what to tick for.

The map on page 5 shows many of the places mentioned in the book. Spanish names have been used for places and people, except where the English names are very well-known.

Some places may be closed during the winter or on certain days of the week. It is a good idea to check opening times with a local tourist office. Look for a sign saying *Oficina de Turismo,* or *Delegación Provincial de Turismo.*

Before your trip it is helpful to collect as much information as you can about the area you are going to visit. On page 61 there is a list of useful addresses and books to read. Don't forget your camera, and a notebook for recording interesting things you see.

You could make a collection of things to remind you of your holiday by saving postcards, bus and entrance tickets, menus, sweet wrappers, small coins and anything else you can find.

Facts about Spain

The official name for Spain is El Estado Español. It covers an area of 504,963km. This includes mainland Spain, the Balearic Islands, the Canary Islands, the cities of Melilla and Ceuta on the coast of North Africa, and some small islands off the coast of Morocco.

History

In the Middle Ages Spain was made up of separate kingdoms, some of which were ruled by the Moors, invaders from North Africa. In 1460 the two strongest kingdoms were united when King Fernando of Aragón married Queen Isabel of Castilla. In 1492 they recaptured southern Spain from the Moors and so united most of Spain.

Languages

The official language is Castillian Spanish, which comes from a mixture of Latin and Arabic. In Cataluña many people speak the Catalán language. The Basque language is spoken in the Basque regions of the Pyrenees, and Gallego in parts of Galicia.

The flag

The red strips are said to represent the blood shed in the country's wars. The yellow represents the gold from South and Central America which made Spain rich.

The king

The head of state is King Juan Carlos de Bourbon. His heir is his eldest son, Felipe.

The government

The government is headed by a prime minister and a council of ministers. The Spanish parliament, the Cortes, has 554 members, and is elected for four years. Spain is divided into 14 main regions, consisting of 50 provinces, each with an assembly and governor.

Main products

Spain's main crops are olives, grapes, oranges, lemons, onions, tomatoes, wheat, barley and sugar beet. Sherry and wine are major exports. Tourism is one of the most important industries.

Facts and figures

Population: 37,000,000
Six largest cities: Madrid, Barcelona, Valencia, Sevilla, Zaragoza, Bilbao
Highest mountain: Teide, Tenerife, 3,718m
Longest river: Ebro, 910km
Official religion: Roman Catholic

4

These islands are off
the coast of Morocco,
over 1000 km from
Spain.

CANARY ISLANDS

Public holidays

1 January: New Year's Day
6 January: Day of the Three Kings
19 March: St Joseph's Day
Maundy Thursday
Good Friday
1 May: Worker's Day
25 May: Corpus Christi

24 June: The King's Saint's Day
25 July: St James' Day
15 August: Assumption Day
12 October: Spanish Day
1 November: All Saints' Day
8 December: Conception Day
25 December: Christmas Day

Shopping, Eating and Money

When you go abroad it is fun to explore the shops to see the different kinds of things they sell. Here are some of the most useful places to shop in Spain. You can find out about smaller shops on page 8.

Some towns in Spain have large supermarkets called **Hipers** or **Supermercados**. These often have stalls outside selling hot food, such as paella.

In the centre of most towns there is a **market** where you can buy all kinds of things, including fresh fruit and fish.

SIMAGO

El Corte Inglés, Galerías Preciados and Simago are department stores which have branches in many towns.

Money

Spanish money is the peseta. Five pesetas are sometimes referred to as one "duro". You can find out how many pesetas there are to the pound or dollar at any bank.

On the **1,000 peseta** note is a picture of José Echegaray, a Spanish scientist, dramatist and politician.

The **500 peseta** note shows Jacinto Verdaguer, a 19th century Catalán poet.

Eating

Cafés are open from early in the morning until very late at night. You can buy snacks and sometimes proper meals. In the evenings, people often entertain their friends in cafés, rather than at home.

Bars (also called *Tascas* and *Tabernas*) serve drinks and snacks called *tapas*. These could include olives and mushrooms or small pieces of seafood.

Look out for restaurants called **Hosterías** or **Fondas**. These serve special regional dishes and sometimes have waitresses in traditional costume.

The **100 peseta** note shows the Spanish composer Manuel de Falla.

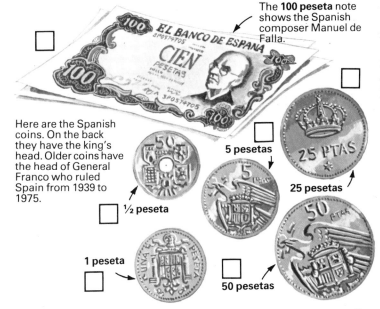

Here are the Spanish coins. On the back they have the king's head. Older coins have the head of General Franco who ruled Spain from 1939 to 1975.

½ peseta

1 peseta

5 pesetas

25 pesetas

50 pesetas

7

The Shops

Pastelería. You can buy cakes, pastries, and sweets here. It sometimes sells wines and spirits too.

Librería. This is a bookshop, not a library.

Churrería. A café where you can have coffee and fritters called *churros*. People sometimes come here for a late breakfast.

Farmacia. The chemist's shop. This is where you buy medicines. Look for the red cross outside.

Carnicería. Butcher's shop. The meat is usually displayed on a glass-fronted refridgerated counter because of the hot weather.

Estanco, Tobacconist's. You can buy stamps here too. Look for the red and yellow sign.

Fruteria. Fruit shop. You will often see the fruit piled outside the shop.

You can often see **balloon sellers** in the street and in parks.

Tienda de Comestibles. A grocer's shop which sells fresh or tinned food, and household goods.

Droguería. You can buy perfumes and toiletries here, but not medicines.

Ferretería. The ironmonger's. You can buy pots and pans and other hardware.

Pescadería. The fishmonger's. You can see the fish displayed on mounds of ice to keep it cool.

Panadería. This sells fresh bread. You can often smell the bread being baked.

Agencia de Viajes. You can buy railway, boat or airline tickets, and book coach tours here.

Tocinería. A special pork butcher's, selling pork, ham, sausages and cooked meats. You can see the different meats hanging from the ceiling.

Oficina de Turismo. Tourist information office. It will give you maps and details of hotels and places to visit.

Correos. Post office. You can have letters sent to you at the *Lista de Correos* in the town where you are staying.

This kiosk sells **newspapers**, **magazines** and **postcards**.

9

Food

Spanish food varies a lot from region to region. It is a mixture of Arabic as well as European styles of cooking. Here are some of the most well-known dishes to look out for.

Gazpacho is a cold soup from Andalucía. You sprinkle pieces of tomato, pepper, cucumber and fried bread into it.

Empanada is from Galicia. It is a pie filled with any kind of meat or fish as well as onions and peppers.

Paella, a speciality of Valencia, is named after the shallow metal pan it is cooked in. It is yellow saffron rice with pork, chicken, fish and shellfish.

Cocido is from Castilla, but you can find it in other parts of Spain too. It is a stew made with different kinds of meat, sausage, chick peas and vegetables.

Fabada is a thick bean soup made with pork, ham and spiced sausage. It comes from the Asturian mountains.

The **tortilla**, a potato omelette, is eaten all over Spain. Sometimes it has onions, and other ingredients too.

Trout stuffed with slices of smoked ham *(jamón serrano)* is a traditional recipe from Navarra.

Riñones al Jeréz are kidneys cooked with sherry. This dish is from Andalucía.

Calamares en su tinta is squid cooked in its own ink. You can find this in all the coastal regions.

Pollo a la Chilindrón is from Aragón It is chicken lightly fried with peppers, tomatoes and olives.

Seafood

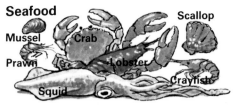

Mussel, Crab, Scallop, Prawn, Lobster, Crayfish, Squid

Seafood is very popular in Spain. There is a good delivery service so that you can often get fresh fish inland too. See how many of these you can spot in restaurants and fishmongers.

Zarzuela de Mariscos is a spicy shellfish stew from Cataluña and Galicia.

Ingredients and flavourings

Olive oil is used a lot in Spanish cooking. Olives are one of Spain's main crops and grow mostly in the south.

In the north you may see **men travelling from door to door, selling garlic and dried peppers**. These are also common ingredients.

Breakfast

Here is a typical **Spanish breakfast**. It consists of *churros* (fritters), *buñuelos* (sugary buns), toast, butter and jam.

Puddings

Two popular puddings are **flan**, which is similar to cream caramel, and **brazo de gitano**, or gypsy's arm, a kind of Swiss roll with rum-flavoured filling.

Sweets and cakes

Spanish sweets and cakes are very sweet, especially in the south, where there was more Arab influence.

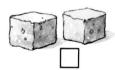

Membrillo is a jelly made from a fruit called a quince.

Yemas are egg yolk sweets traditionally made by the nuns of San Leandro, Andalucía.

Marzipan animals are often sold at Christmas, Easter and other festivals.

Drinks

Spain is famous for its **sherry** – a wine strengthened with brandy. It is named after the English pronunciation of Jerez de la Frontera, where it is made. Other countries make sherry too, but real sherry comes from the area around Jerez. There are two main types: Fino (pale and dry) and Oloroso (dark and sweet).

Spain produces many different types of wine. One of the best and most expensive is from the **Rioja** region.

Spanish children often drink **Blanco y Negro** – black coffee with a spoonful of vanilla ice cream.

Sangría is a popular refreshing drink, made from red wine, brandy, fruit, sugar, soda water and ice.

A **porrón** is a special container for drinking wine. Pour the wine into your mouth from about half a metre, trying not to spill it.

Cremat is a strong Catalán drink, made from rum, gin, coffee, sugar and lemon. It is set alight as it is served.

Horchata is a sweet milky drink, made from crushed almonds. It comes from the south-east of Spain.

Newspapers, Magazines and Crafts

Here are some different magazines and newspapers to look out for when you are in Spain.

Vanguardia, Arriba and **El País** are the main national daily papers. In Cataluña, look out for **Avui** and **Punt Diari**, which are written in the Catalán language.

There are several weekly news magazines, such as **Semana, Destino, Actualidad** and **Gaceta Ilustrada**. Pulgarcito and T.B.O. are children's comics.

Crafts

There are a number of traditional crafts still carried out in Spain. Here are some that you can buy.

Most regions have their own style of pottery. This is from Valencia.

Lace and embroidery

Hand-made Spanish **guitars**.

Basket and wickerwork

Jewellery. This is a traditional design from Toledo.

Leather goods are cheaper in Spain than in many places.

Roads and Transport

Motorways in Spain are called *Autopistas* and are marked as "A" roads on the map. Main roads, or *Carreteras Nacionales,* are marked with a red "N" on the map. *Carreteras Radiales* are special roads linking Madrid with main cities or frontiers.

Autopistas de peaje are motorways where you have to pay a toll. They were built privately and the toll helps pay for the building and maintenance. You pay the money at kiosks like this built across the motorway.

The motorways have **special service areas**. This board shows that you can buy food, drink and petrol.

There is only one brand of petrol in Spain – **CAMPSA**. It comes in three grades: normal, super and extra.

On some parts of the motorway there are **rest areas**, with trees, tables and benches and pieces of sculpture.

Signs

Warning signs are painted on triangles with red edges. This one – beware of falling rocks – is common in the Pyrenees.

All vehicles used for commercial purposes, such as taxis, display an **SP plate**. It stands for *servicio público*.

Lorries, caravans and trailers have special **numbers on the back** which show the maximum permitted speed.

Madrid and Barcelona both have an underground system called the **Metro**. Look out for this sign.

What the signs mean

CUIDADO/PRECAUTION   Caution
DESPACIO   Slow
DESVÍO   Diversion
PASO PROHIBIDO   No thoroughfare
CURVA PELIGROSA   Dangerous bend
DIRECCIÓN ÚNICA   One way street
PELIGRO   Danger
ESTACIONAMIENTO PROHIBIDO   No parking
LLEVAR LA DERECHA   Drive on the right
LLEVAR LA IZQUIERDA   Drive on the left
ESTACIONAMIENTO
DE AUTOMÓVILES   Car park

Vehicles to spot

SEAT 133. Popular two-door car. Made in Spain under licence from the Italian company FIAT.

Taxi. It has a coloured stripe down the side, and a light on the roof to show that it is for hire.

Ambulance. Usually privately run converted Citroën estate cars. Equipped for most emergencies.

Fire engine. There are several different models in use, but they are all red with blue flashing lights.

Water tanker. In some areas pure drinking water is not available. Spring water is delivered in tankers.

Butane gas delivery truck. Many families use butane gas for cooking. It comes in orange cylinders.

Trains

Spanish railways, the RENFE, operate many different kinds of trains. *Omnibuses and ferrobuses* are slow local trains. The TER, the TAF and the *Talgo* are fast trains for which you pay special supplements. On some days, *Días Azules,* you can get reductions for children. Ask at the local station.

Look out for the **Talgo**, a type of very fast diesel train built in 1950. It has reclining seats and air-conditioning. The trains are silver and have special names, such as the "Virgen de Lourdes".

Buses

Spanish **buses** are single-decked. You give the driver your fare as you enter, and leave by a door in the middle. There are few seats so most people stand.

Planes

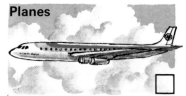

Iberia is Spain's national airline. The planes are painted with the national colours and are all named – DC10s are called after Spanish painters.

15

In the Countryside

Here are some things to spot as you travel through the countryside. Some things will vary according to what part of Spain you are in. The crops that are grown depend on the climate and soil. Try to recognize the most common local crop.

In the south you will see a lot of **olive plantations** Olives grow well in areas with little rainfall.

There are **vineyards** in many parts of Spain. In September you can see the grapes being harvested.

Look out for bright yellow fields full of **sunflowers** They are grown to make oil.

In many places you can see people **threshing corn** in the traditional way. The farmer rides on a sledge pulled by horses which are treading on the corn to separate the grains.

Rice is grown near Valencia. The fields are irrigated by canals. Canal gates are opened and closed to control the amount of water going to each field.

It is quite common to see huge **advertisement hoardings** in the middle of fields. This bull is advertising a make of brandy and sherry.

Fruit

Almond

Pomegranate

Orange

Date

Fig

Water melon

Prickly pear

There are many different types of fruit grown in Spain. Here are some of the most common ones you will see.

Things to spot

Look out for different kinds of **windmills,** such as the ones from La Mancha (left) or the one from Cadíz (right). Some have been mechanized and are still in use.

A noria is a well with a wheel which has small buckets attached to it. A donkey is tied to the wheel. As it walks round, water is drawn up in the buckets.

In central Spain, you sometimes see **storks** nesting in the chimney pots.

In the corn-growing areas of the north, you can see **hórreos,** which are used for storing grain. They are built of stone or wicker, and stand on columns topped with flat stones, to prevent rats climbing in.

Look out for **rows of poplars** along modern or deserted roads. They were originally planted by the Romans.

You can find **religious shrines** in remote places, such as on mountain paths.

In Galicia, **granite crosses** are a common sight. Some have Christ carved on them.

Sometimes you will see **donkeys laden with special panniers** for carrying things.

Sometimes you can see **women carrying things on their heads,** such as milk churns or heavy baskets.

Heavy loads of hay or vegetables are often carried on a **cart drawn by a pair of yoked oxen.**

Beaches

This map shows you the different Spanish coasts, and tells you what their names mean.

Costa Verde
green coast

Costa Brava
rugged coast

Costa Dorada
golden coast

Costa de Azahar
orange blossom coast

Costa Blanca
white coast

Costa de la Luz
coast of light

Costa del Sol
coast of the sun

Canary Islands

These islands are off the coast of Morocco, over 1000 km from Spain.

Where to eat

Most beaches have a **merendero** – a stall selling drinks and ice creams.

You can often find small open-air restaurants called **chiringuitos**.

Things for hire

Many beaches have **sunshades** for hire.

Sometimes there are **beach chairs** too.

Changing tents are especially common on the north coast.

What to do

Along the Costa Brava and Costa Dorada there are tourist boats called **cruceros**. They cruise along the coasts or travel from one resort to another.

Some of these boats have **glass bottoms**. You can travel over the reefs to see the colourful fish and plant life.

You can go for **camel rides** in the Canary Islands. Some beaches have black sand. This is caused by volcanic eruptions.

On most beaches you can hire a two-seater paddleboat called a **pedalo**. This costs about 100 pesetas an hour.

You can often hire small **sailing dinghies** for about 300 pesetas an hour.

Snorkelling equipment is quite cheap to buy. Even in shallow water you may see unusual fish, plants and coral.

Windsurfing is a popular new sport, but it is not suitable for young children.

Things to spot

You often see **coconut sellers** on Spanish beaches

On the north west coast you may see **hórreos**, which are used for storing grain.

These unusual looking boats are for **catching mussels**. They have wires dipping into the sea which mussels cling to.

Houses

Traditional styles of Spanish houses vary from region to region, according to the different climate and the building materials that are available. Here are some of the main types. See how many you can spot.

In the pine-growing regions of central Spain, houses are often made from a mixture of **wood and plaster**, though the ground floor is stone. These houses are from Ciudad Real in La Mancha.

Around Valencia you can see houses called **barracas**, with steep thatched roofs. The walls are made from strips of poplar bark mixed with clay and straw.

In the south there are **flat-roofed, white-washed houses,** similar to ones in North Africa. They are made of stone as there are very few trees.

Farmhouses

Cortijos are Andalusian farmsteads. The farmer and his workforce live in a group of houses built round a central courtyard. Many of the farms are for breeding horses or bulls.

In the Basque regions, look out for **caseríos**. They are made from wood and stone and have wide sloping slate roofs with overhanging eaves. There is often a south-facing balcony. Farm animals sleep on the ground floor.

Masías are Catalán country houses with two or three storeys. The top floor is used for storing grain.

Town houses

In La Coruña on the north coast you can see **houses with balconies enclosed with glass**. This helps keep out the wind and rain. Pedestrians keep dry by walking along the arcades beneath the houses.

In the towns in the north many people live in flats in **tall narrow houses with large balconies.**

The towns in the south are sometimes called the "**white towns**" because the houses are whitewashed. They have thick walls and small windows to keep them cool. As there is little rain, the roofs are flat or gently sloping.

Unusual houses

In some places in the south, such as Almanzora or Guadix, there are gypsies living in **cave houses**. Notice the chimney pots and television aerials sticking out of the ground.

At Cuenca in central Spain there are some interesting **hanging houses** which are balanced on the side of a cliff. They are about 600 years old.

House Details

Most Spanish houses do not have front or back gardens. In the afternoons and evenings you often see **people sitting on chairs in the street**.

The southern houses have a **patio** in the centre, with palms or potted plants. In Córdoba there is an annual competition to choose the best one.

Houses in the south often have **pots of flowers hanging on the outside walls**. This is the Street of the Flowers in Córdoba.

Look out for decorated tiles, or **azulejos**, on the walls. Many houses have tiles on the floors too.

In northern Spain look out for **shields and coats of arms** above doorways.

Most houses have **shutters**. This type is rolled up at the top of the window.

Sometimes you see **red peppers hanging from rooftops or doorways** to dry.

Ironwork

Spain is famous for its designs in wrought iron. Look out for interesting **decorated balconies**.

There is usually a **decorated iron gate** leading into the patio.

Iron bars against the windows, called **rejas**, let air in and protect the house from intruders.

Towns and Villages

There are a lot of old towns and villages in Spain. In the Middle Ages, villages were often built so that they could be easily defended. Here are some examples of different types of towns and villages you might see.

In Castilla you can often see **villages built round castles on hilltops**. The castle is probably in ruins now, but it once provided work for the villagers.

In the south there are **villages built on steep cliffsides**. This made them difficult to attack. Sometimes the rock forms the outside walls of the houses.

Some towns, such as Toledo, are **built on the bend of a river**. The river provided water and a good defence against enemies.

Walled towns, such as Avila, were built in the Middle Ages. The Avila walls are still complete. They have 88 towers and nine gateways.

Some towns have one or two old **gateways** still standing. This used to be the only way in and out of the town.

Old towns on the coast are usually **ports or fishing towns**. Cádiz was founded in 1100 by Phoenician traders from North Africa.

Sometimes you see old **villages built round a church**. Religion played a central part in people's lives and the church was often the most important building.

23

Visiting Towns and Villages

There may be a **statue** of a king or important local person. This is the explorer Pizarro, who discovered Peru.

In the centre of the oldest part of a town or village you can find a main square, usually called the **Plaza Mayor**. It often has trees and seats where people meet to talk.

Look out for different kinds of **stone crosses**.

Religious shrines are sometimes built into the side of a wall. People leave flowers and lighted candles.

Some towns have **interesting street lamps** made of decorated wrought iron.

Some houses do not have running water. So people do their washing in a special **communal washing area**.

There are often **taps or wells** in the main square. See how many different types you can spot.

Look out, too, for interesting **fountains**. Some have **carved animals' heads** with water coming out of their mouths.

As it is very hot in the south, the streets are often narrow to help keep out the sun. Sometimes a **canopy** is hung between the houses to make extra shade.

In many parts of Spain the pavement is in an **arcade** beneath the first floor of the buildings. This is a protection against hot as well as damp weather.

Look out for **paintings** and **graffiti** on the walls. This one is advertising the Spanish Communist party.

Some cafés have a **grapevine shading the tables**. It is supported by a canopy made of netting.

The local **cemetery** is usually just outside the village and surrounded by high walls.

Street sellers

In Spain a lot of things are sold in the street, partly because of the warm climate. Here are some examples.

Lottery tickets – often sold by the blind or disabled.

. **Turrón** – a kind of nougat.

A stall selling **fresh orange juice**.

Policemen's uniforms

These are the **Policía Armada,** who carry guns and guard official buildings.

The **Guardias Civiles** patrol in cars or on motorbikes, or work as customs officers.

The **Urbanos** are traffic police. Their uniforms are blue in winter and white in summer.

Prehistoric Spain

There were people living in caves and rock shelters in Spain over 30,000 years ago. Spain has lots of painted caves – mostly in the Cantabrian Mountains in the north and along the Mediterranean coast. Find out at your local tourist office which caves you can visit. There are a number of other prehistoric remains to see too.

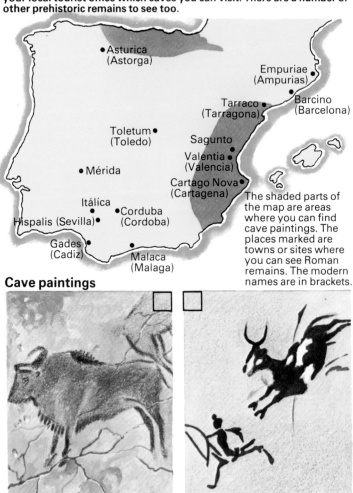

- Asturica (Astorga)
- Empuriae (Ampurias)
- Tarraco (Tarragona)
- Barcino (Barcelona)
- Toletum (Toledo)
- Sagunto
- Valentia (Valencia)
- Cartago Nova (Cartagena)
- Mérida
- Itálica
- Corduba (Cordoba)
- Hispalis (Sevilla)
- Gades (Cadiz)
- Malaca (Malaga)

The shaded parts of the map are areas where you can find cave paintings. The places marked are towns or sites where you can see Roman remains. The modern names are in brackets.

Cave paintings

The **northern cave paintings** are the oldest. Some are 30,000 years old. They show the animals people used to hunt – deer, boar and bison. The most famous caves, at Altamira*, are closed.

The **cave paintings on the east coast** are about 12,000 to 15,000 years old. These show human figures and scenes, such as hunting. This is known as the "Second Hunter" style.

26   *You can see reproductions of these paintings, see page 40*

Cave signs and symbols

Here are some of the signs and symbols found drawn in the caves.

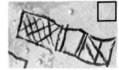

The **Indalo**. This symbolized a legendary giant from the region of Almería.

The **Tectiform**. This may have been a symbol for a building or animal trap.

Outlines of human hands. These were found in some caves.

Dolmens are tombs made from large stone slabs. There are several of these in the region of Antequera. This is the Cueva de Menga, near Antequera.

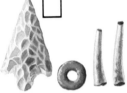

Prehistoric **weapons and tools** were made from hard stone called flint. **Jewellery** was made from shells and teeth with holes bored in them.

Iberian Spain

The period of about the last 1,000 years BC is known as the Iberian period. Archeologists have discovered sculptures, painted pottery and elaborate gold and metalwork. The Iberians traded with the Phoenicians from North Africa, who brought Greek, Egyptian and Syrian goods with them. The Celts came to Spain in about 700BC and the Greeks in about 500BC, so archeological finds show many different styles.

The **Dama de Elche** is one of the most famous pieces of Iberian sculpture. You can see it in the Prado Museum in Madrid.

The Iberians also made carvings of animals. These are the **Bulls of Guisando**, at El Tiemblo, near Avila.

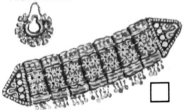

A lot of **gold jewellery** has been discovered in the south of Spain. It is thought to have come from the legendary city of Tartessos.

Roman Spain

The Romans invaded Spain in 218BC. They built roads all over the country and many modern roads follow the same routes. They set up irrigation systems and worked mines. There are a number of Roman remains to see. On page 26 there is a map showing where the best sites are.

At Itálica near Sevilla, are the remains of a large **Roman town**. It was the birthplace of the Emperor Hadrian. You can see where the streets and houses used to be. There are some mosaics and the fourth largest amphitheatre in the world.

Roman theatres were semicircular. The best-preserved theatre is at Mérida, where plays are still performed. The stage consists of a set of marble columns with statues between them.

Amphitheatres were round arenas surrounded by seats. Here the Romans used to hold chariot races and gladiator fights.

The Romans invented the arch, which meant they could build stronger, higher bridges. There are several **Roman bridges** in Spain. This one is at Alcántara.

Aqueducts were used to carry water from one place to another. The Segovia aqueduct, built in the 1st century AD, is 300 metres long and brought water from the Sierra Fonfría, 14 kilometres away.

Roman temples were elaborately carved. This one at Mérida was dedicated to Mars, the god of War.

Roman arches in Spain were usually built in memory of an important person. This one is at Medinaceli.

Mausoleums were burial places for rich people. This one at Fabara was dedicated to the spirits of the ancestors.

Cemeteries were always built outside towns. The Tower of Scipios, near Tarragona, is the tomb of a noblewoman.

In some towns you can see the remains of **Roman walls**, though often they have been added to at later periods.

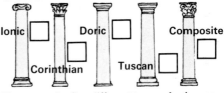

Ionic   Doric   Composite

Corinthian   Tuscan

These are the five different types of **columns** used in Roman archiecture. See how many you can spot. The Ionic and Corinthian were originally Greek, and the Doric was adapted from the Greek version.

Mosaics are pictures or patterns made from small coloured stones. They were used to decorate floors. Some are scenes from everyday life, others show legends.

Look out for Roman remains in local museums. They may have **coins, pottery, statues or ornaments** that have been dug up in the area.

Moorish Spain

The Moors were Muslims from North Africa, who came to Spain in 711AD and ruled parts of the country until 1492. They brought science and maths skills and introduced paper and also the numbers we use today. They also planted orange and lemon trees. You can still see Moorish style architecture, especially in the south.

The **Alhambra** is a Moorish city built on a hill in Granada. It includes two luxurious palaces, which were begun in the 12th century. Between 1236 and 1492 the Alhambra was the capital of Muslim Spain. You can visit it on any day of the week.

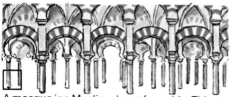

A **mosque** is a Muslim place of worship. This one at Córdoba was the most important in Spain. It is now a cathedral. Notice the horseshoe arches and stripes of red brick and white stone. These are typical Moorish features.

The Moors built beautiful **gardens** with pools and fountains. These are the gardens of the Partal in the Alhambra.

Look out for **minarets** – towers for calling people to prayer – which were built next to mosques. This one is the Giralda in Sevilla.

Spotting Moorish styles

Moorish ideas had an influence on building styles in Spain. Churches built by refugees from Muslim Spain are called "Mozarabic". Buildings constructed by Muslim craftsmen after the Christians reconquered Spain are known as "Mudejar".

The Moors sometimes used overlapping **multifoil arches**. These are made up of lots of little arches.

Some churches copied **Moorish ceilings with parallel ribs**. Sometimes the ribs overlapped to form a star shape.

The Moors often built in **brick**. Look out for brick churches and other buildings, especially in Castilla and Aragón.

Mudejar craftsmen built **belfries** that looked like minarets. Some are decorated with patterns in brick and coloured tiles.

Decoration

The Moors carved intricate designs in the plaster on walls. The Koran, the Muslim holy book, forbade the representation of people or animals. Patterns were based on **geometric shapes** (left), **plants** (centre) or **Arabic writing** (right).

Carved wooden ceilings are called **artesonados**. You can see this elaborate "honeycomb" ceiling in the Alhambra.

Moorish walls and floors were sometimes decorated with **mosaics** made from pieces of coloured pottery, or **tiles**. Many modern houses have similar tiles.

Some Moorish words are still used in Spain. Look out for **words beginning with "A" or "Al"**, such as alcázar, meaning castle. These often have Moorish origins.

Churches

Here are some of the different styles of churches you will see in Spain, and some clues to finding out how old they are. They are often a mixture of styles as they have been added to at different periods. Old Spanish churches are often well preserved because of the mild climate.

Asturian (700s–800s) Narrow with round arches. Found in the province of Asturias.

Mozarabic (800s–900s) Built by refugees from the Muslim parts of Spain. Look out for the horseshoe arches.

Romanesque (1000s–1100s) Thick stone walls with towers. Round arches on doors, windows and vaults.

Route of the pilgrims

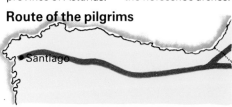

You can see a lot of Romanesque churches along this road. It was the **route of the pilgrims**, who came from France to visit the tomb of Santiago (St James). This pilgrimage was one of the most important in the Middle Ages.

Gothic (1100s–1500s) A lot of cathedrals, such as Burgos (above), were built at this time. Tall, with a lot of windows and spires. Pointed arches.

Baroque (1590s and 1600s) Very elaborate style. Many older churches, such as the cathedral at Santiago de Compostela (above), were rebuilt with Baroque fronts.

Parts of a church

Mozarabic horseshoe arch

Romanesque round arch

Gothic pointed arch

Many Spanish churches have **richly carved doorways**. This is the Portico de Gloria at the cathedral of Santiago de Compostela.

In the 1500s walls were often decorated with delicate carvings. This style is called **Plateresque**, as it looked like the work of a *platero*, or silversmith.

Romanesque barrel vault. Rounded with a series of arches.

Gothic rib vault. Tall arches meeting at a point.

Stellar vaulting. 1500s dome with star shape made from thin strips of stone.

In some Romanesque churches you can still see **frescoes**, pictures painted straight onto the wet plaster of walls. These are from San Isidoro, León.

Stained glass windows

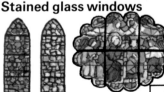

Stained glass windows, often showing scenes from the Bible, were introduced in the Gothic period. See how many different shaped windows you can spot.

33

Things to spot in Churches

In the 16th century Spain was very wealthy because of the gold and other treasures brought back from South America. A lot of this wealth was spent on churches, which are often highly decorated inside and have elaborately carved objects, such as statues. Here are some things you could look out for when you visit a Spanish church.

The **coro**, or choir, is where the priests pray. Notice the carved wooden seats, called choir stalls.

The entrance to the *coro* often has an iron grill, or **reja**. Some are painted with gold leaf and have intricate designs.

A **reredos** or a **retablo** is a painted or carved screen at the back of the altar. Many of these are enormous.

Some churches have a collection of treasures, such as **jewelled crosses**, or cups called **chalices**.

Rich or famous people often have **carved tombs**. Look out for unusual poses. This knight is reading a book.

Decorated chests are usually used for storing valuable things, or vestments – the clothes that priests wear in church.

Sometimes you can visit the **crypt**, an underground room beneath cathedrals and large churches.

Cloisters are covered arcades round a courtyard. You can find them in churches that were once attached to monasteries. Spanish cloisters are often decorated with carvings of saints or scenes from the bible.

Castles 1

Spain has about 1,500 medieval castles. There are a lot in the region of Castilla, which was named after the word *Castillo,* meaning castle. Here are a few of the castles you can visit. They are usually open every day from 9 a.m. to 1 p.m. and from 3 p.m. to 7 p.m.

Segovia Castle looks like a fairy-tale castle. It dates back to the 12th century, but was mostly rebuilt in the 19th century. You can visit the throne room, the royal bedrooms and an armoury, where you can see old canons, lances and crossbows.

The **Alcázar at Almeria** is an Arab fortress, begun in the 8th century. It once housed 20,000 men. You can see a ruined palace, gardens, baths and dungeons.

The **Castle of Loarre** in Huesca dates back to the 11th century. It was the home of an order of fighting monks and the nobles who they fought for.

Belmonte Castle is a 15th century castle built by the Marquess of Villena. It is six-sided with lots of circular towers. Inside there are elaborate ceilings.

Coca Castle is a very ornate 15th century Moorish Style castle, made of pink brick. It was built as a home for the archbishop of Sevilla.

Castles 2

Most Spanish castles were built between the 8th century, when the Moors invaded, and the 15th century, when Spain became united under King Fernando and Queen Isabel. The style of a castle varies according to when it was built, though they were often added to at different periods. Here are some examples of different types of castles and some features to look out for.

Moorish castles date from the 8th century. Many have square towers and sharply pointed battlements. This one is at Almodóvar del Rio.

Early castles in the south (800s–1100s) usually have an inner and an outer wall, with square or many-sided towers. They are made of stone, brick or cement mixed with pebbles.

Early Christian castles in the north copied the ones in the south. They are made of rubble, which was the only material available, and the towers are round or semicircular.

Most **14th and 15th century castles** were built by nobles who wanted to protect their land from the king. You can usually find them in strong positions on hilltops. They fit the landscape and so are irregular in shape.

Fortified palaces, such as Manzanares el Real, date from the middle of the 15th century. These were built as homes rather than places to be defended, and are often highly decorated, outside as well as inside.

Things to spot in castles

Bartizan turret. Small round room sticking out from top of wall or tower. Used for watching for enemies.

Machicolations. Holes beneath the battlements through which things could be dropped on enemies.

Loop-holes. Narrow slits in walls through which arrows could be shot while the archers remained safe.

Wall-walks are walk-ways behind the battlements, which connect the towers.

Drawbridge. A bridge across a moat which could be raised from inside as enemies approached

Portcullis. Strong iron gate which slides up and down. Used for blocking the entrance to a castle.

Wedge-shaped towers. These were introduced by the Moors and can be found in south and central Spain.

Look out for **noble coats of arms** carved on the walls.

The insides of castles were often decorated by Mudejar craftsmen. Some have **elaborately carved ceilings**.

Castles you can stay in

Keep a look out for **armour and weapons** on display.

Some castles have been converted into **Paradors** – hotels run by the government. You can find out about these at your local tourist office.

37

Madrid

Madrid became the capital of Spain in 1561. It is built on a plateau 654m above sea level in the centre of the country. The summers are very hot and the winters very cold. A small river, the Manzanares runs through the city. Madrid has over three million inhabitants.

In the 16th and 17th centuries, heretics were burnt in the **Plaza Mayor** by the Spanish Inquisition. It was also used for plays and pageants. People used to watch the events in the square from their balconies.

The **Arco de Cuchilleros** is one of the entrances to the square. Here is the sign of the restaurant "Cuevas de Luis Candelas", named after a famous highwayman.

The Puerta del Sol is the centre of the old city. There is a **statue of a bear and tree**. They are the symbols of Madrid.

Outside the police headquarters in the square is the **Kilómetro Cero**, the point from which all distances in Spain are measured.

In the **Plaza de España** is a monument to the popular Spanish writer Cervantes, and his two best-known characters, Don Quijote and Sancho Panza.

The **Puerta de Alcalá** was built in 1778 in honour of Charles III. A tax on wine was raised to help pay for it.

The Spanish parliament, **the Cortes**, was built in 1850. The bronze lions were made from the metal of enemy cannons.

The **Cibeles Fountain** in the Calle Alcalá shows Cibeles, the Greek goddess of fertility, riding a chariot drawn by lions. It was built in the 18th century.

The **Calle Alcalá** and the **Avenida de San José**, or **Gran Vía**, are the two major shopping streets. Look out for Grassy's jewellery store which has a clock museum.

The **Rastro** is a busy open-air market, selling antiques, junk, toys and old clothes. You can find it on Ribera de Curtidores Street.

On Sunday mornings there is a **stamp collectors market** in the Plaza Mayor.

The **Church of San Jerónimo** built in the 16th century, is where many royal marriages have taken place.

The Post Office, or **Palacio de Communicaciones**, is a huge building, a bit like a cathedral. People often meet here.

The **university** is built in enormous grounds just outside Madrid. It was modelled on an American campus.

Places to visit near Madrid

The **Escorial** is a very large palace and monastery 49km from Madrid. It was built by Philip II after his victory at the battle of St Quentin in 1557.

Franco is buried at the **Valle de los Caídos**, a memorial to the Spanish Civil War. There is a church carved inside the hill.

What to see and do in Madrid

The Royal Palace

The **Royal Palace** was built for Charles III on the site of a castle which was burnt in 1734. On a few days it is closed and used for state ceremonies.

There are luxurious rooms to visit, such as the **throne room**. You can also see a museum of old carriages, an armoury, the crown jewels, and an old pharmacy.

Interesting museums

The **Prado*** is one of the world's greatest art museums. It has a lot of famous paintings by Spanish artists, such as the one on the right.

This is the **Maids of Honour** by Velázquez.

The **Museo de América*** has a collection of toys, dolls, masks and other things that the Spaniards brought back when they invaded South and Central America.

The **Archeological Museum*** has reproductions of the cave paintings at Altamira, which are 30,000 years old.

The **Colon Wax Museum*** has figures of famous people and scenes from fantasy and horror stories. Some of them have special sound and light effects.

You can visit the **Royal Tapestry Factory*** and watch tapestries being made. It was started in 1721 and Goya created many of the original designs.

You can see old coins and banknotes at the **Money Museum***, which is above the mint where money is actually made.

The **Museo del Pueblo Español*** has costumes and old household objects from different regions of Spain.

You can visit the 4th century BC **Debod Temple***. It was rescued from Egypt to stop it being flooded when the Aswan Dam was built.

At the **Railway Museum*** you can see interesting models of old trains.

You can see a collection of old weapons and armour at the **Army Museum***.

The **Naval Museum*** has model ships, old maps and instruments used on board ship.

Parks

The **Retiro Park** was built by Philip II. It has fountains, rose gardens and a huge lake for boating.

Casa de Campo is the biggest park in Madrid. It has a zoo, a huge wood, a lake, and a funfair.

You can travel to the funfair by **cable car** from Paseo del Pintor Rosales street.

The **Botanical Gardens** has 30,000 species of plants and trees from all over the world.

Barcelona

Barcelona is the capital of Cataluña and the second most important city in Spain. It is the largest port and a centre of banking, publishing and industry. The city was founded by the Carthaginians from North Africa about 1,700 years ago. The oldest part is nearest the sea and is known as the "Gothic quarter". The "Ensanche", or modern city, was designed in the last century by Cerda, an engineer, who also designed part of Stockholm in Sweden. Here are some suggestions of things to see and do in Barcelona.

The **cathedral**, which lies in the centre of the Gothic quarter, dates back to the 13th century. At midday on Sundays, local people gather outside to dance the Sardana, a traditional Catalán dance.

The **Sagrada Familia** church, designed by the Barcelona architect Gaudí, was begun in 1884 and is still unfinished. It is sometimes called the "Sandcastle Cathedral".

The **Plaza de Cataluña** is the centre of Barcelona. It has fountains, statues and a flower clock.

This is the **Palacio de la Diputación**, which was the old parliament when Cataluña was a separate kingdom.

The 19th century **Gran Teatro del Liceo** is the second largest theatre in the world, after La Scala in Milan.

In the **Plaza Nueva** you can see Roman pillars and a building with designs by the Spanish artist Picasso on it.

42

The **Ramblas** is a wide tree-lined avenue that runs from the waterfront to the city centre. It has open-air stalls which sell flowers, books, newspapers and caged birds.

In the **Plaza Real** there are some unusual street lamps designed by Gaudí. Stamp collectors meet here on Sunday mornings.

The **Plaza del Rey** is a historic square where it is said that King Fernando and Queen Isabel received Christopher Columbus on his return from America.

The waterfront

You can go by lift to the top of the **Columbus memorial** for a good view of the harbour.

Between 9 a.m. and sunset you can go on board a replica of the **Santa María** – the boat in which Columbus sailed to America.

In the port area, the **Barceloneta**, you can see lots of different boats, and people mending fishing nets.

You can go for **trips round the harbour** in special sightseeing boats.

What to see and do in Barcelona

There are two mountains in Barcelona – Montjuich and Tibidabo. You can travel to the top of them by **funicular railway**.

They both have **funfairs** which are open all the year round.

On Montjuich you can explore the **Pueblo Español** – an artificial village which has styles of architecture from all the regions of Spain. It was built for a world exhibition held in Barcelona in 1929.

Inside the village there are lots of small craft shops where you can watch **potters and glass-blowers** at work.

For a good view of the old part of Barcelona you can travel by **cable car** from Montjuich to the port.

Montjuich park has lots of unusual fountains. This illuminated one is lit up on Sundays and public holidays.

Some travel agencies in Barcelona organize **donkey rides** (*burro safaris*) and trips into the country on horse and cart (*tartana*).

Güell park is a fairy-tale park designed by Gaudí. It is full of strange-shaped buildings, pillars and mosaics.

Ciudadela Park has lots of different kinds of sculpture, such as the lady and the umbrella fountain and a stone mammoth.

Inside the park you can find **Barcelona Zoo,** which has a good collection of unusual animals, such as the white gorilla "Snowflake"

Interesting museums

The **Picasso Museum*** has the world's largest collection of pictures by the Spanish artist Picasso.

The remains of ancient Roman Barcelona are on show in the basement of the **Museo de Historia de la Ciudad***

At the **Museo de Indumentaria*** you can see all kinds of costumes from the 16th century to the present.

The **Museo de Cera*** has wax models of famous people from history and fiction. This is General Franco.

You can see guns, toy soldiers and uniforms at the **Museo Militar*** in the old fort on Montjuich mountain.

The **Maritime Museum*** is inside a shipyard which was built in 1378 and is the oldest in Europe.

*You can find out the addresses on page 61.

Sports and Bullfighting

Football

Real Madrid have won the European Cup six times. The **players** usually wear all white.

Football is the most popular spectator sport in Spain. Matches are held on Sunday eveings between October and May. This is **Santiago Bernabeu**, the home stadium of Real Madrid, Spain's most famous team.

This is the **club emblem**. *Real* means Royal. King Alfonso XIII gave them this title in 1920.

Pelota is a fast moving Basque game, played in a court called a frontón. There are four players. Each has a curved basket, or *cesta,* to throw and catch the ball. Spectators bet on the winners during the match.

Long distance cycling races go on for days and attract large audiences. One of the most famous is the Vuelta a Cataluña, which starts in Barcelona.

Rowing regattas are held on the north coast. The boats are stronger and more difficult to steer than the ones used for river racing.

Sports you can do

Skiing is very popular. The main areas are the Pyrenees, the Guadarrama mountains, the Sierra Nevada mountains, and Manzaneda in Galicia.

In most tourist areas you can hire **tennis** courts for about 200 pesetas an hour. In other parts of Spain you may need to join a private club.

You will need a licence if you want to go **fishing**. To apply for one, ask at the tourist office, or at the local branch of ICONA, a conservation organization.

Spain has many good quality **golf** courses. Some are used for international tournaments, such as the Canada Cup, and the Eisenhower Trophy.

Bullfighting

The bullfight or **Corrida** takes place on Sunday evenings. The origins of bullfighting go back to legends of the Persian god, Mithras, who killed bulls.

It is performed in several stages. There are six bulls and three main bullfighters, or matadors, who wear brightly coloured, embroidered costumes.

Festivals 1

There are lots of festivals, or fiestas, in Spain. Even the smallest villages have one. Most of them celebrate religious feast days. People sometimes wear traditional costumes, and there are fireworks, processions, bullfights and dancing in the streets.

Easter

Holy Week, the week before Easter, is celebrated all over Spain. On **Good Friday**, statues of saints or scenes from the crucifixion are carried through the streets on floats, or *pasos*, lit by candles. The processions in Sevilla (above) are especially famous.

These men are called **Penitents**. They belong to "brotherhoods", which originate from the medieval trade guilds. Each brotherhood has its own colours.

Many of the **statues** are very valuable as they are decorated with jewels. The Virgin of the Macarena (above) was carved in the 17th century.

In Alberique, you can visit the **statues in people's houses**. They are taken from the church for Holy Week. Visitors are welcome for a drink and a *buñelo* (a bun).

On **Easter Saturday** in Cataluña you may see young people in the street singing and collecting money or sweets. They often have baskets and a decorated donkey.

Other religious festivals

Corpus Christi in June is celebrated in many towns. At Sitges, people make patterns in the streets with flowers. Prizes are given for the best designs.

On Assumption Day (15 August) a religious play, **the Misteri**, is performed at Elche. Singers and musicians strapped to a cable are lowered from the church dome.

Assumption Day is celebrated in other towns too. The fiesta at La Alberca lasts about four days, with dancing and a street play.

Verbenas take place the night before a religious feast. There are fireworks and buildings are strung with ribbons and flags.

Romerías are picnic outings to a saint's shrine. They are held in country districts. The most famous is to El Rocío at Whitsun. People arrive on horseback or in white covered wagons decorated with flowers. They sing and play the guitar and castanets.

Festivals 2

The **Fiesta of San Fermín** is held in Pamplona from 6 to 15 July. Each day there is the *Encierro*, when bulls run through the streets to the bullring. People run ahead to prove their courage. Most years somebody is injured.

There are several fiestas in which **mock battles between the Moors and the Christians** are acted out. They are mostly in southern Spain. One of the most famous is at Alcoy on 23 April.

At **Christmas** it is traditional to eat *turrón* – a kind of nougat made from honey and almonds.

On **New Year's Eve**, to bring good luck, it is the custom to eat 12 grapes as the clock strikes midnight – one for each chime.

Spanish children receive their presents on **6 January**. They leave their shoes out on the balcony the night before.

In Madrid and some other towns there is a **parade of the three kings,** who ride camels or horses through the streets.

The **Fallas of Valencia** are held from 12 to 19 March. People make huge figures or scenes from wood, rags and papier-mâché. The figures are usually of topical subjects or caricatures of local politicians or well-known people. On 19 March, the best one is chosen and the rest are burnt.

Some towns, such as Sevilla (above), have **Ferias**, which were originally horse or cattle markets. People wear traditional costumes, and there are parades of horses and carriages. Some people hire *casetas* – small enclosures – for private parties.

In September there are **fiestas of the vendimia**, or grape harvest, in grape-growing regions. These men are treading the grapes in the traditional way.

Many large towns have a **summer festival**. All kinds of events are organized, including music, sport, tree-felling competitions and gazpacho tasting.

51

Things to look out for at Festivals

During a fiesta, people often give each other small presents. There are **street stalls** selling toys, sweets and small gifts.

At many fiestas there are **Gigantes** (giants) or **Cabezudos** (huge papier-mâché heads). They often represent people from history. These ones are of King Fernando and Queen Isabel.

In the Basque region you may hear **Bersolaris**. These are men who shout mock rhyming abuse at each other from opposite sides of the street.

Costumes

Here are the head-dresses from some of the regional costumes. They are often worn at fiestas. See if you can spot any of them.

The traditional **mantilla** and comb from Andalucía.

Embroidered bonnet from Cáceres.

Peinata from Valencia.

Veil from Almería in southern Spain.

Hat and veil from Logroño in Castilla.

Straw bonnet from Tenerife, Canary Islands.

Music and Dancing

The **Flamenco** dance is from Andalucía and is probably of Gypsy or Arabic origin. It is usually accompanied by the guitar and castanets.

Tuna singers are students who sing and play the guitar or mandolin at fiestas, and in restaurants and hotels. They began in the 16th century and wear the costume of that time.

In Cataluña you may see **Castellers**, who perform a dance by standing on each other's shoulders to make a tower.

This is the **Aurresku**, a Basque dance. Each dancer tries to leap higher than the others.

The **tamboril**, a side drum, and the **txistu**, a kind of flute, are Basque instruments.

On 21 and 22 July at Anguiano in Logroño, you can watch people doing a **stilt dance**.

The **Jota** is a lively dance which comes from Aragón. It is rather like a jig.

The **gaita** is a small version of Scottish bagpipes, played in north-western Spain.

In Cataluña, in the summer, you can watch **Sardana** dancing competitions.

53

Fun Things to do 1

At **Tabernas**, near Almería, you can walk through the streets of sets used to make cowboy films. This is a very arid area with dramatic scenery. There are huge cracks in the earth and hardly any trees or plants. It is often used for Westerns and films set in the desert, such as *Lawrence of Arabia*.

Touring sherry cellars

In the region of Jerez de la Frontera, you can go on **tours of the bodegas**, or cellars, where sherry is stored. You can see the processes used for making sherry and sample some different types. To find out about tours contact the local tourist office.

In September, when they are harvested, you can see **grapes drying** in the fields on straw mats.

This is a **grape-press**. Years ago grapes were pressed by men trampling on them wearing special boots.

To sample the sherry the glasses are filled with a **venencia**, a bendy piece of bone with a silver cup.

This is the **Enchanted City** near Cuenca. Weather has worn away the rocks and left strange shapes. Many of them have names, such as "the elephant" or "the man's face".

In the main square at Olot in Cataluña there is a **huge chess board** with giant pieces. The pieces are kept in a wooden box at the edge of the square and anyone can play.

You can see into the garden of **Salvador Dali's strange house** at Port Lligat, Cadaqués. There are all kinds of sculptures, including giant eggs and faces. Dali is a famous Spanish painter.

There is a very unusual tree at Icod on the island of Tenerife. It is called the **Dragon Tree** and is supposed to be 3,000 years old. There are a few other trees like it, but not as old.

Things to watch

In the evenings, in fishing towns such as Garrucha in Almería, you can watch **fish being auctioned** to the shopkeepers and the public.

At midday on Thursdays outside Valencia Cathedral, the **Water Tribunal** meet to solve disputes concerning the watering of crops. This custom is 600 years old.

Fun Things to do 2

There are several exiting **caves** to visit in Spain. The Drach (or Dragon) caves in Mallorca are among the most famous limestone caves in the world.

They are nearly three kilometres long. You enter by boat from the sea, and there are coloured lights so you can see the stalagmites and stalactites.

Fun ways to travel

You can go by **cable car** to the top of the Teide volcano in Tenerife, and see small puffs of white smoke coming from the crater.

At Benidorm and some other towns on the coast a few **steam trains** have been restored and painted, and you can go for rides along the old tracks.

At Mijas on the Costa del Sol you can hire a **donkey,** or *burro,* taxi, though it can be expensive.

In some towns, such as Sevilla, you can go for sightseeing trips in an old-fashioned **horse and carriage**.

From Pontevedra you can hire a **boat to the island of Ons**. The people there speak the Gallego language.

Watching people at work

Many factories and craft workshops will let you come and watch people at work. Sometimes you have to arrange your visit in advance, which you can do at the local tourist office. But keep a look out for small craft shops. They will usually let you in without an appointment.

In the region of La Mancha, you can often see women sitting out in the street **making lace**.

In Toledo you can visit a workshop where they make **steel goods,** such as knives or swords, decorated with gold, and black.

Potters are often happy to let you watch them at the wheel or painting designs on the pots.

At Easter time you can watch **bakers** making castles, spaceships and all kinds of shapes from chocolate.

At Manacor on the island of Mallorca you can visit a factory where they make cultured **pearls**.

In most parts of Spain you can still find workshops where there are people **weaving** on hand-operated looms.

Circuses

Look out for posters advertising travelling **circuses**. They usually perform in the local bullring which has a canopy put up over it.

Funfairs

There are mobile **funfairs** that travel round the country too. They usually come to a town when it has a fiesta.

Fun Things to do 3

Parks

In the **Botanical Gardens in Valencia** there is a play area with a roadway which has an old railway engine, a tram and other machines to play on. There is also a small zoo with monkeys.

At Elche near Alicante you can see the only **palm forest** in Europe. Look for the amazing "Imperial Palm" which has seven arms.

National parks

Parques Nacionales (national parks) are areas of beautiful countryside where animals and plants are protected. There are eight of them in Spain. This is the Aigües Tortes Park.

At the **Covadonga National Park** there is a wide variety of animals including bears, wolves, wild cats, squirrels, badgers and foxes.

At **Rioleón Safari Park***, near Vendrell, Tarragona, you can see wild animals roaming free, and performing lions and dolphins. You can go tobogganing on a special slideway too.

Interesting museums

There are lots of museums to visit in Spain. In most areas you can find an archeological museum or a museum of the history of the region or town. Here are some of the more unusual museums you could visit.

In Sitges there is an interesting **toy museum** called the Lola Anglada. It has a collection of dolls from all over the world dating back to the 17th century, as well as other toys.

At the **Falla Museum** in Valencia, you can see the best Fallas* from each year. Fallas are papier-mâché models made every year for the feast of St Joseph.

Also in Valencia is the **National Pottery Museum** where you can see brightly coloured pottery and tiles. This is a reconstruction of an old Valencian kitchen.

The **Casa de Dulcinea**, El Toboso, Toledo is a museum about Don Quijote, who was invented by the Spanish writer Cervantes. Quijote wore armour and fought windmills because he thought they were giants.

There is a **wine museum** at Vilafranca del Penedés. It shows wine-making equipment from the time of the Ancient Egyptians. You will be given a glass of wine to try at the end.

At Vitoria is the unique **Museo de Naipes**, which is a museum of playing cards. The cards come from all over the world and some are over 500 years old.

At the **Pontevedra Museum** you can see an exhibition about hórreos. Hórreos are now used for storing grain, but some very old ones were the homes of the ancient Celts, over 2,000 years ago.

*For more about Fallas, see page 51

Car Number-Plate Game

The first letters on Spanish car number-plates tell you which province they come from. As you spot the letters, colour in the map.

A	Alicante	GE	Gerona	P	Palencia
AB	Albecete	GR	Granada	PM	Baleares
AL	Almería	GU	Guadalajara	PO	Pontevedra
AV	Ávila	H	Huelva	S	Santander
B	Barcelona	HU	Huesca	SA	Salamanca
BA	Badajoz	J	Jaén	SE	Sevilla
BI	Viscaya	L	Lérida	SG	Segovia
BU	Burgos	LE	León	SO	Soria
C	La Coruña	LO	Logroño	SS	Guipuzcoa
CA	Cádiz	LU	Lugo	T	Tarragona
CC	Caceres	M	Madrid	TE	Teruel
CE	Ceuta	MA	Málaga	TF	Tenerife
CO	Córdoba	ML	Melilla	TO	Toledo
CR	Ciudad Real	MU	Murcia	V	Valencia
CS	Castellón	NA	Navarra	VA	Valladolid
CU	Cuenca	O	Oviedo	Z	Zaragoza
GC	Las Palmas	OR	Orense	ZA	Zamora

Useful Addresses

The Spanish National Tourist Office (S.N.T.O.) will supply lists of hotels, *paradores,* campsites and details of tours. They also provide leaflets about different towns and provinces of Spain. There are also booklets telling you about winter sports, golf, fishing and other things to do on holiday in Spain.

Spanish National Tourist Office, 57 St James St, London SW1. tel: (01) 499 0901.

In U.S.A.: 589 Fifth Avenue, New York, N.Y. 10017. tel: (212) 759-3842.

In Canada; 60 Bloor Street West, Suite 201, Toronto 5, Ontario. tel: (416) 961-3131.

For general information on Spain, you can contact the **Spanish Institute,** 102 Eaton Square, London SW1. tel: (01) 235 1485.

Guide books and phrase books

The *Michelin* green guide, the *Blue* guide and *Fodor's Spain* are all good basic guides to Spain, listing interesting things to see and place to visit in the different towns and regions. Some other guide books are listed below.

You will have much more fun on holiday if you can speak some Spanish, so it is a good idea to take a phrase book too.

Letts go to Spain (Letts)
Discovering Spain (Harrap)
Costa del Sol and Andalusia (Berlitz)
Costa Dorada and Barcelona (Berlitz)
Madrid (Berlitz)
Junior Guide to Spanish (Usborne).

Museums

Colon Wax Museum, Paseo de Calvo Sotelo, 41, Madrid. tel: 419 22 82
Army Museum, Mendez Nuñez, 1, Madrid. tel: 221 67 10
Railway Museum, San Cosme y San Damián, 1, Madrid. tel: 467 34 91
Archeological Museum, Serrano 13, Madrid. tel: 226 68 32
Prado Museum, Paseo del Prado, Madrid. tel: 468 09 50
Royal Tapestry Factory, Fuenterrabia, 2, Madrid.
Naval Museum, Montalbán, 2, Madrid. tel: 221 04 19
Debod Temple, General Fanjul Gardens, Madrid.
Museo de América, Avenida de los Reyes Católicos, 6, Madrid.
Money Museum, Doctor Esquerdo, 36, Madrid.
Museo del Pueblo Español, Plaza de Marina Española, Madrid.
Museo de Cera, Rambla de Santa Mónica, 4, Barcelona. tel: 317 2649.

Picasso Museum, Calle de Montcada, 15, Barcelona.
Museum Militar, Montjuich Castle, Barcelona.
Maritime Museum, Reales Ataranzanas, Puerta de la Paz, Barcelona.
Museo de Historia de la Ciudad, Casa Clariana-Pardellás, Plaza del Rey, Barcelona.
Museo de Indumentaria, Palacio del Marqués de Llío, Calle de Montcada, Barcelona.

Zoos and Safari Parks

Zoo Municipal de Fuengirola, Camino de Santiago, Fuengirola, near Málaga.
Rioleón Safari Park, Albiñana, near Vendrell, Tarragona.
Auto Safari Andaluz, Finca La Alcaidesa, San Roque, Cádiz.
Jardín Zoologico y Botánico 'Alberto Durán', Jardínes de Tempul, Jerez de la Frontera.

Index

PRINTED IN BELGIUM BY
proost
INTERNATIONAL BOOK PRODUCTION

Part 2

SPANISH PHRASES

and how to say them

Contents of Part 2

How to use this Part of the Book

This book will help you make yourself understood in most everyday situations when you are on holiday or travelling in Spain. The phrases have been kept as simple as possible, and include some of the possible answers to the questions you may want to ask. There are also translations of many of the signs you will see.

The book is divided into sections, each covering a situation you are likely to find yourself in. Use the contents list at the front or the index at the back to help you find the pages you need. You will find it easier if you look up the section you are going to need in advance, so you can practise saying the phrases.

For most phrases, there is a picture with a speech bubble containing the Spanish. Underneath the picture is a guide to help you pronounce the Spanish and an English translation. Like this:

Hablo español.

Abloh espan-yoll.
I can speak Spanish

On the next two pages, you will find out how to use the pronunciation guide and there are some useful hints and phrases to remember. At the back of the book you can find some very basic Spanish grammar, including a few common verbs.

Points to remember

We have not always had enough space to include the words for "please" (por favor), or "excuse me" (perdone). Try to remember to add them when you are asking for things.

Por favor

There are four words in Spanish for "you" – tú, vosotros, usted and ustedes. Tú (singular) and vosotros (plural) are used by close friends and children. Usted (singular) and ustedes (plural) are for speaking to people you don't know very well. Be careful about using tú or vosotros, as people may think you are being rude.

Tú or Usted?

67

Pronunciation Guide

We have tried to keep the pronunciation guides in this book as simple as possible. For each Spanish sound we have used the English word, or part of a word, which sounds most like it. Read the pronunciation guide in what seems to be the most obvious way. It will sound better if you say it quickly, so it is a good idea to practise a bit. People should be able to understand what you are saying, even if you won't sound quite like a Spanish person. If you want to learn really good pronunciation you should try to find a Spanish person to teach you.

Here are some general points to remember when you are trying to speak Spanish.

A mark like this above a vowel is called a "stress mark". It means you should stress this part of the word more than the rest.

A mark like this above an "n" gives it a nasal sound, rather like "ny". Pronounce it as you would in the English word "new".

The Spanish "h" is never pronounced. All the other letters are pronounced, except the "u", which is sometimes silent.

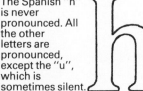

Vowels, especially "o", sound better if you say them without closing your mouth at the end of the sound. Many consonants, such as "d", sound softer than in English.

The Spanish "r" is made by putting your tongue behind your top teeth. Think of the "r" in "grrr...!", the sound of a dog growling.

The Spanish "j" is a bit like an English "h". To pronounce it, you make a sound rather like the one you make when you gargle.

The letters "b" and "v" sound the same in Spanish. To pronounce them, make a sound half-way between the two.

In Spanish, "ll" is pronounced like the second part of the word "million", or like a "y", as in "yellow".

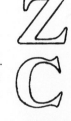

The Spanish "z" is pronounced "th". "C" also has a "th" sound, when it is followed by an "i" or an "e". Otherwise it is pronounced as in the English word "cat".

In Spanish "qu" sounds like "k", as the "u" is silent.

Some Basic Words and Phrases

Here are some useful words and phrases which you will need in all kinds of situations.

Sí	No
See	No
Yes	**No**

Por favor	Gracias
Pour favorr	Grathee-ass
Please	**Thank you**

Buenos días
Booenoss dee-ass
Hello

Adiós
Addy-oss
Goodbye

Lo siento
Lo see-entoh
I'm sorry

Perdone
Peardonay
Excuse me

Señor
Sen-yorr
Mr

Señora
Sen-yorra
Mrs

Señorita
Sen-yorreeta
Miss

Some simple questions

How much?	¿Cuánto? Cwantoe?
Why?	¿Por qué? Pour kay?
Which one?	¿Cuál? Cwal?
Where is . . .?	¿Dónde está . . .? Donday esta . . .?
When?	¿Cuándo? Cwandoe?
Have you?	¿Tiene usted . . .? Tee-enay oo-sted . . .?
Is or are there . . .?	Hay . . .? ¿Eye . . .?

Some simple statements

I am . . .	Soy or Estoy . . . Soy or Estoy . . .
I have . . .	Tengo . . . Tengo . . .
It is . . .	Es or está . . . Ess or esta . . .
It is here.	Está aquí. Esta a-key.
It is there.	Está allí. Esta eye-ee.
This one.	Este. Estay.
That one.	Ese or aquél. Essay or a-kell.
I would like . . .	Me gustaría . . . May goostar-reeya . . .

Problems with the language

Do you speak English?
¿Habla usted inglés?
Ab-la oo-sted ingless?

I do not speak Spanish
No hablo español.
No abloh espan-yoll.

I do not understand.
No entiendo.
No entee-endoh.

Please speak more slowly.
Más despacio, por favor.
Mass desspathy-oh pour favorr.

What does that mean?
¿Qué quiere decir?
Kay kee-airray deth-earr?

Finding your Way

¿La estación, por favor?

La estatheeon, pour favorr.
How do I get to the railway station, please?

Tiene que tomar el autobús número cinco.

Tee-enay kay tomarr el out-oh-boos noomairroh thing-co.
You must take a number 5 bus.

¿Dónde está la parada del autobús de El Escorial?

Donday esta la pa-ra-da del out-oh-boos day El Es-corry-al?
Where is the bus stop for El Escorial?

Allí. Es aquélla.

Eye-ee. Ess a-kay-ya.
Over there. It's that one.

¿Es ésta la parada de El Escorial?

Ess esta la pa-ra-da day El Es-corry-al?
Is this where I get off for El Escorial?

Por favor. ¿Dónde está el castillo?

Pour favorr. Donday esta el casteeyo?
Where is the castle, please?

Perdone. Me he perdido. ¿Cómo se llama esta calle?

Peardonay. May ay peardeedo. Com-o say ya-ma esta ky-yay?
Excuse me. I'm lost. What is the name of this street?

¿Me lo enseña en el mapa, por favor?

May lo ensenya en el ma-pa pour favorr?
Can you show me on the map?

General directions

Tuerza a la derecha.
Twertha a la derecha.
Turn right.

Tuerza a la izquierda.
Twertha a la eethkee-airda.
Turn left.

Todo recto.
Tohdoh recktoh.
Go straight on.

 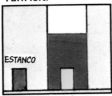 

Está enfrente del cine.
Esta enfrentay del theenay.
It's opposite the cinema.

Está al lado del estanco.
Esta al lahdoh del estangco.
It's next to the tobacconists.

Está en la esquina.
Esta en la eskeena.
It's on the corner.

 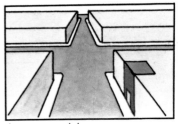

Está nada más al pasar el puente.
Esta na-da mass el pass-are el pwentay.
It's just after the bridge.

Justo antes del cruce.
Hustoe antess del crewthay.
It's just before the crossroads.

Some places to ask for

la estación
la estatheeon
railway station

el aeropuerto
el airopwertoe
airport

la comisaría
la comisareeya
police station

el banco
el bangco
bank

las tiendas
lass tee-endass
the shops

71

At the Railway Station

¿Dónde se compran los billetes?

Allá, al fondo, en el despacho de billetes.

Donday say compran loss bee-yetess?
Where can I buy a ticket?

Eye-ya, al fondoe, en el despatchoe day bee-yetess.
Over there, at the ticket office.

¿Cuánto cuesta un billete para Madrid?

Un billete de ida para Madrid.

Dos billetes de ida y vuelta para Madrid.

Cwantoe cwesta oon bee-yetay pa-ra Madreeth?
How much is it to Madrid?

Oon bee-yetay day eeda pa-ra Madreeth.
One single ticket to Madrid.

Doss bee-yetess day eeda ee vwelta pa-ra Madreeth.
Two return tickets to Madrid.

¿De qué andén sale el tren para Madrid?

Andén número 5.

Day kay anden salay el tren pa-ra Madreeth?
Which platform does the Madrid train leave from?

Anden noomairroh thing-co.
Platform five.

¿A qué hora sale el tren?

Ah kay orra salay el tren?
What time does the train leave?

¿Es éste el tren para Madrid?

Ess estay el tren pa-ra Madreeth?
Is this the Madrid train?

¡He perdido mi billete!

Ay peardeedoh me bee-yetay!
I've lost my ticket!

¿A qué hora llega el tren de Valencia?

Ah kay orra yay-ga el tren day Valentheea?
What time does the train from Valencia arrive?

¡Mozo!

Mohthoh!
Porter!

Information

Luggage collection

Waiting room

Lost property

Main line trains

Suburban trains

Left luggage

Not drinking water

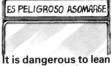

It is dangerous to lean out of the window

Travelling by Car

¿Dónde está el garage más cercano?

Donday esta el garah-hay mass thairr-canoh?
Where is the nearest garage?

¿Cuánta gasolina quiere?

Cwanta gasoleena kee-airray?
How much petrol do you want?

Llénelo, por favor.

Yenayloe, pour favorr.
Fill it up please.

¿Puede comprobar el aceite y el agua?

Pweday comprobar el athay-eetay ee el agwa?
Can you check the oil and water?

He tenido una averia.

Ay teneedo oona avair-reeya.
I have broken down.

¿Qué le pasa?

Kay lay passa?
What's the trouble?

Los frenos no andan bien.

Loss fraynoss no andan beeyen.
The brakes are not working properly.

Quiero alquilar un coche para esta semana.

Kee-airroh alkee-lar oon cochay pa-ra esta sem-ahna.
I would like to hire a car for the week.

Parts of the car

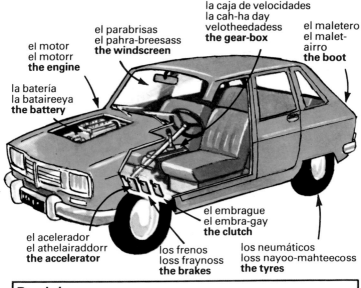

el motor
el motorr
the engine

la batería
la bataireeya
the battery

el parabrisas
el pahra-breesass
the windscreen

la caja de velocidades
la cah-ha day
velotheedadess
the gear-box

el maletero
el malet-
airro
the boot

el acelerador
el athelairaddorr
the accelerator

los frenos
loss fraynoss
the brakes

el embrague
el embra-gay
the clutch

los neumáticos
loss nayoo-mahteecoss
the tyres

Road signs

Found in forests and dry areas. Warns of the danger of fire.

Beware of the train.

Give way to other cars.

Restricted parking area. You need a blue disc to park here.

Motorway toll 1000m away.

Entrance to car park.

Town centre this way.

This shows you the coastal resorts you can get to from the next turn off.

At the Hotel

Hotels are graded from one to five stars, and prices are controlled by the government. You can get lists of hotels from a tourist office. Look out for *paradores* – first class hotels run by the government. These are often in converted castles or monasteries, or in places with beautiful scenery.

Booking in advance

Me gustaría reservar una habitación para la semana que viene.

May goostar-reeya resairvar oona abeetatheeon pa-ra la sem-ahna kay vee-enay.
I would like to book a room for next week.

Finding a room

Lo siento muchísimo, pero el hotel está completo.

Lo see-entoh moocheesy-mo, pear-o el ohtell esta completoh.
I'm sorry but the hotel is full.

¿Puede aconsejarme otro hotel?

Pweday aconsayhahmay oh-troe ohtell?
Can you recommend another hotel.

Una habitación con dos camas.

Oona abeetatheeon con doss camass.
A room with two beds.

Una habitación doble con baño.

Oona abeetatheeon doblay con banyo.
A double room with bathroom.

Una habitación individual con ducha.

Oona abeetatheeon individ-ooal con doo-cha.
A single room with shower.

¿Cuánto tiempo piensa quedarse?

Cwantoe tee-empoh pee-ensa kaydarr-say?
How long will you be staying?

Hotel Meals

Lista de Precios

Habitación con desayuno
Bed and breakfast

Habitación con desayuno y cena
Half board

Pensión completa
Full board

¿A qué hora sirven el desayuno (el almuerzo, la cena)?

A kay orra seer-ven el des-eye-oonoh (el almoo-airthoe, la thayna)?
What time is breakfast (lunch, dinner) served?

Huevos fritos
Oo-evoss freetoss
Fried eggs

Tostadas
Toh-star-dass
Toast

Chocolate con churros
Chocolahtay con chew-rross
Chocolate with fritters

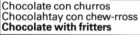

¿Pueden prepararme la comida en bocadillos?

Pweden preparahmay la comeeda en bocka-deeyoss?
Could you make me a packed lunch?

Mi llave, por favor.

¿Cuál es el número de su habitación?

Me ya-vay pour favorr.
My key, please.

Cwal ess el noomairroh day soo abeetatheeon?
What is your room number?

Me gustaría dejar un recado para mi hermano.

May goostar-reeya dayhar oon reckahdoe pa-ra me airrmanoh.
I would like to leave a message for my brother.

Paying the bill

¿Podría prepararme la cuenta?

Podreea preparahmay la cwenta?
My bill, please.

Going Camping

There are over 500 campsites in Spain – mostly along the coast. They often have good facilities, such as swimming pools, sports areas, restaurants and supermarkets. You can get a list of approved campsites from the Spanish Tourist Office.

Finding a campsite

¿Se puede acampar aquí?

Say pweday a-camp-are a-key?
May we camp here?

Perdone. ¿Hay un camping cerca de aquí?

Peardonay. Eye oon campeeng therka day a-key?
Is there a campsite near here?

Tenemos una caravana y dos tiendas.

Tenaymoss oona ca-ra-vana ee doss tee-endass.
We have a caravan and two tents.

At the campsite

Nos gustaría quedarnos una semana.

Noss goostar-reeya kaydarnoss oona sem-ahna.
We would like to stay a week.

¿Tienen un lugar a la sombra?

Tee-enen oon loo-gar a la sombra?
Have you a place in the shade?

¿Hay otras familias inglesas?

Eye ohtras fameeleeass inglessass?
Are there any other English families here?

¿A qué hora cierran por la tarde?

Ah kay orra thee-airran pour la tarrday?
What time do you close in the evenings?

¿Dónde me puedo lavar?

Donday may pwedoh lahvar?
Where can I wash?

¿Dónde hay agua?

Donday eye agwa?
Where can I find some water?

Perdone. ¿Puedo usar su linterna?

Peardonay. Pwedoh oosarr soo lintairr-na?
May I borrow your torch?

Perdone. ¿Podemos encender una hoguera?

Peardonay. ¿Podaymoss enthendair oona ogairra?
Are we allowed to make a camp fire?

¿Qué es ese olor?

Kay ess essay olorr?
What is that smell?

Por favor. ¿Pueden hacer un poco menos de ruido?

Pour favorr. Pweden athair oon pohcoh menoss day roo-eedoh?
Please could you make less noise.

What the signs mean

SE PROHIBE FREGAR LOS PLATOS EN LOS LAVABOS.
No washing up in the basins.

APARCAMIENTO OBLIGATORIO
Compulsory parking

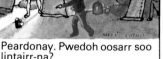

AGUA POTABLE
Drinking water

RESERVADO PARA CARAVANAS
Caravans only

SE RUEGA A LOS CAMPISTAS ECHEN LA BASURA EN LOS RECIPIENTES PREVISTOS PARA TAL FUNCION.
Campers are requested to dispose of their rubbish in the places provided.

Going Shopping

Most Spanish shops are open from 9.00 a.m. to 7.00 p.m. They close for a long lunch break between 1.00 p.m. and 4.00 p.m. Big department stores are usually open at lunchtime, but they open later in the morning and close earlier in the evening.

Perdone, ¿dónde puedo comprar fruta?

Peardonay, ¿donday pwedoh comprarr froota?
Where can I buy some fruit?

¿Tiene manzanas?

Tee-enay manthan-ass?
Have you any apples?

¿Cuántas quiere?

Un kilo.

Cwantass kee-airray?
How many would you like?

Oon keeloe.
A kilo.

Cuatro lonjas de jamón, por favor.

Cwatroe long-has day ham-on pour favorr.
Four slices of ham, please.

Estoy mirando.

Estoy me-randoe.
I am just looking.

Signs

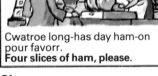

Saldos

Sale

Auto-Servicio

Self service

ASCENSOR

Lift

Abierto de las 9 a las 6·30

Open from 9 a.m. to 6.30 p.m.

Buying clothes

¿Haría el favor de enseñarme una camisa estampada?

Ahreeya el favorr day ensenyarmay oona cameesa estam-pada?
Can you help me? I am looking for a patterned shirt.

Sí. ¿Qué talla desea?

See. Kay tie-ya dessay-a?
Yes. What size do you want?

¿Puedo probármela?

Pwedoh probarmayla?
May I try it on?

Es demasiado grande.

Es demasiado pequeña.

Es dem-assee-addoh granday.
It's too big.

Es dem-assee-addoh pek-ayn-ya.
It's too small.

¿Cuánto es?

Cwantoe ess?
How much is it?

¿Tienen algo más barato?

Tee-enen algo mass ba-ratoh?
Have you anything cheaper?

¿Dónde pago?

Donday pag-oh?
Where do I pay?

Gracias.

De nada.

Grathee-ass.
Thank you.

Day na-da.
You are welcome.

The Shops 1

Ultramarinos · Alimentación
Ooltra-mareenoss - Alleementatheeon **Grocers**

Querría . . .

Care-reeya . . .
I would like . . .

algunas conservas
algoonass con-sair-vass
some tinned foods

queso
kayzoh
cheese

mantequilla
mantay-keeya
butter

huevos
oo-ev-oss
eggs

mermelada
mair-mel-adder
jam

té
tay
tea

leche
laychay
milk

azúcar
a-thoo-car
sugar

galletas
ga-yet-ass
biscuits

miel
me-ell
honey

mostaza
mos-tath-a
mustard

café
caf-ay
coffee

judías verdes
who-deeass vair-dess
green beans

guisantes
geese-antess
peas

coliflor
collyfloor
cauliflower

patatas
pa-ta-tass
potatoes

lechuga
le-chew-ga
lettuce

champiñones
champin-yoness
mushrooms

frambuesas
framboo-esass
raspberries

coles
coless
cabbage

tomates
tom-at-ess
tomatoes

cebollas
thebo-yass
onions

un limón
oon lee-mon
a lemon

manzanas
manthan-ass
apples

peras
pear-ass
pears

una naranja
oona na-ranha
an orange

ciruelas
theerooay-lass
plums

fresas
fressass
strawberries

plátanos
plat-a-noss
bananas

82

CARNICERÍA

Carneethair-reeya
Butcher

carne picada de vaca
carnay pikada day va-ca
minced beef

un pollo
oon po-yo
a chicken

un bistec
oon beestek
a steak

chuletas
de cordero
chew-letass
day cordairro
lamb chops

Charcutería

Sharcootair-reeya
Pork Butcher

longanizas
longan-eethass
sausages

chuletas de cerdo
chew-letass day
thairdoe
pork chops

foie grass
fwa-gra
paté

salchichón
salcheechon
salami

entremeses
entray-messess
**prepared salads
and cooked meats**

Panadería

Panaddair-reeya
Baker

unos bollos
oonoss bo-yos
some rolls

pan
pan
bread

una barra de pan
oona barra day pan
a long loaf

PASTELERÍA

Pastelair-reeya
Cake and Sweet Shop

una tarta de frutas
oona tarta day frootass
a fruit tart

unos caramelos
oonass ca-rramelloss
some sweets

un pastel
oon passtell
a cake

PESCADERÍA

Pescadair-reeya
Fishmonger

lenguado
leng-gwa-doe
sole

una gamba
oona gamba
a prawn

merluza
mair-lootha
hake

bacalao
back-allow
cod

The Shops 2
Librería · Papelería · Kiosco

Leebrair-reeya – Papelair-reeya – Key-oskoe
Bookshop – Stationers – Newspaper kiosk

tinta
tin-ta
ink

un bolígrafo
oon bollygraffoh
a ballpoint

un libro
oon leebroe
a book

una goma
oona gom-a
a rubber

sobres
so-brays
envelopes

un lápiz
oon lapeeth
a pencil

un periódico
oon perryoddy-coe
a newspaper

papel para cartas
papel pa-ra cartass
writing paper

un mechero
oon may-chair-roe
a lighter

ESTANCO

Estangco
Tobacconist

un paquete de cigarrillos
oon packetay day theegarree-oss
a packet of cigarettes

cerillas
ther-ee-yas
matches

sellos
say-yoss
stamps

boutique

Booteek
Clothes Shop

una camisa
oona cameesa
a shirt

un sombrero
oon sombrairroh
a hat

unos pantalones cortos
oonoss pantal-oness cor-toss
some shorts

una falda
oona falda
a skirt

un vestido
oon vesteedoe
a dress

unos zapatos
oonoss thapatoss
some shoes

unas sandalias
oonass sandall-yass
some sandals

un jersey
oon hair-say
a jersey

unos pantalones
oonoss panta-
lone-ays
some trousers

un traje de baño
oon trah-hay day ban-yo
a bathing costume

un impermeable
oon im-pear-me-ablay
a raincoat

FERRETERÍA

Fair-retair-reeya
Ironmongers-Hardware Store

un abrelatas
oon abray-la-tass
a tin opener

una linterna
oona lintairr-na
a torch

un destornillador
oon destornee-yadoor
a screwdriver

un sacacorchos
oon sack-a-corchoss
a corkscrew

una pila
oona peel-a
a battery

una bombilla
oona bom-bee-ya
a light bulb

cuerda
cwairda
string

unas tijeras
oonass tee-hair-ass
some scissors

detergente
det-airr-hentay
some detergent

hilo
eel-oh
cotton

una aguja
oona agoo-ha
a needle

un enchufe
oon enchewfay
a plug

gas
gas
Camping gas

FARMACIA

Farmatheeya
Chemist

insecticida
insecteetheeda
insect repellent

jabón
ha-bon
soap

aspirinas
asspeareenass
aspirins

una venda
oona ven-da
a bandage

un cepillo para
los dientes
oon thep-eeyo pa-ra
los dee-entess
a toothbrush

polvos de talco
pol-voss day tal-co
talcum powder

pasta de dientes
passtah day dee-entess
toothpaste

una película
oona peleek-oola
a film

unas tiritas
oonass tiree-tass
sticking plaster

un peine
oon pay-e-nay
a comb

un rollo de papel higiénico
oon rohyo day papel ee-hyen-icoe
a roll of toilet paper

85

Posting a Letter . . .

The post office is called *correos y telégrafos.* It is open from 9 a.m. to 1.30 p.m. and from 4 p.m. to 7 p.m. from Monday to Saturday. You can buy stamps from an *estanco,* or tobacconist's, too. To post letters abroad, look for a box marked *extranjero.*

Perdone. ¿Cuánto es para Inglaterra?

Perdonay. Cwantoe ess pa-ra Inglatairra?
Excuse me. How much is it to England?

Quiero cuatro sellos para Inglaterra.

Key-airroh cwatroe say-yoss pa-ra Inglatairra.
I would like four stamps to England.

Perdone. ¿Dónde hay un buzón?

Peardonay. Donday eye oon boothon?
Excuse me, where can I find a postbox.

The post office

¿Dónde está correos?

Donday esta corray-oss?
Where is the post office?

Quiero mandar un telegrama a Inglaterra.

Key-airroh man-darr oon telaygrama ah Inglatairra.
I would like to send a telegram to England.

Rellene esta ficha, por favor.

Reh-yaynay esta feecha, pour favorr.
Fill in this form, please.

¿Cuánto es por palabra?

Cwantoe ess pour pal-abra?
How much is it per word?

. . . and Changing Money

¿Cuánto es el franqueo de este paquete para Inglaterra?

Cwantoe ess el frankayoh day estay pah-ketay pa-ra Inglatairra?
How much will it cost to send this parcel to England?

¿A qué hora es la última recogida de correo?

Ah kay orra ess la oolteema reh-coh-heeda day corray-oh?
What time does the last post leave?

Signs

POR AVIÓN
Air mail

Paquetes
Parcels

TELEGRAMAS
Telegrams

SELLOS
Postage stamps

Changing money

You can change money and traveller's cheques in a bank, a *cambio* (exchange office) and in some hotels and railway stations. Remember to take your passport with you. Banks are usually open from 9.00 a.m. to 2.00 p.m. *Cambios* are open for longer – sometimes even on Sundays.

Perdone, ¿cambian cheques de viaje?

Peardonay, cam-beean check-ays day veeah-hay?
Excuse me, do you cash traveller's cheques?

¿A cuánto está la libra?

Ah cwanto esta la lee-bra?
How many pesetas are there to the pound?

Por favor, podría darme el cambio en monedas.

Pour favorr, podreea darrmay el cambeeoh en mon-aidass.
Could I have some small change.

Going to a Café

Cafés in Spain stay open from early in the morning to very late at night. You can buy snacks and both alcoholic and non-alcoholic drinks. Many cafés have tables outside, because of the warm climate. Look out for *tapas,* titbits served at the bar to eat with your drinks.

¿Está ocupada?

Esta ocoo-pa-da?
Is this table taken?

¿Qué desean?

Kay dessayan?
What can I get you?

¿Por favor, puede traernos la lista?

Pour favorr, pweday try-airnoss la leesta?
Please may we see the menu.

¿Qué bocadillos tienen?

Jamón, queso y salchichón.

Kay bocka-deeyoss tee-enen?
What sandwiches have you got?

Ham-on, kayzoh ee salcheechon.
Ham, cheese and salami.

Yo quiero dos bocadillos de jamón, una coca cola y un zumo de naranja.

Yo key-airroh doss bocka-deeyoss day ham-on, oona cocka coala ee oon thoomoh day na-ranha.
I would like two ham sandwiches, a coca cola and an orange juice.

Un tenedor, por favor.

Oon tenedorr, pour favorr.
A fork, please.

Un cuchillo
Oon coocheeyo
A knife

Una jarra de agua
Oona harra
day agwa
A jug of water

Yo no he pedido esto.

Yo no ay pedee-doh estoh.
I didn't order this.

Una cuchara
Oona coochara
A spoon

Un vaso
Oon vahsoh
A glass

Una servilleta
Oona sairveeyeta
A napkin

Sal y pimienta
Sal ee peamy-
enta
Salt and pepper

¿Dónde están los servicios?

Donday es-tan loss sairveetheeoss?
Where are the toilets?

¡Camarero!

Cama-rair-roh!
Waiter!

La cuenta, por favor.

La cwenta, pour favorr.
The bill, please.

¿Está el servicio incluido?

Esta el sairveetheeoh in-clue-eedoh?
Is service included?

Going to a Restaurant

Spanish restaurants are divided into categories indicated by the number of forks shown outside – from one to five. Look out for restaurants called *fondas*, *posadas* or *ventas*. These offer good simple meals at reasonable prices.

Querría reservar una mesa para cuatro a las ocho de la tarde.

Care-reeya resairvarr oona messa pa-ra cwatroe a lass och-oh day la tarrday.
I would like to book a table for four at 8 p.m.

¿Tiene una mesa para cuatro?

Tee-enay oona messa pa-ra cwatroe?
Have you a table for four?

¿Ha reservado?

Ah resairrvadoe?
Have you booked?

¿Tiene una mesa al aire libre?

Tee-enay oona messa al eye-ray leebray?
Have you a table outside?

¿Qué desean ustedes?

Kay dessayan oo-stedays?
What would you like to order?

¿Cómo se hace este plato?

Com-o say athay estay platoh?
How is this dish made?

¿Tiene algo muy sencillo?

Tee-enay algo mwee sentheeyo?
Have you got anything plainer?

Drinks

¿Puedo ver la lista de vinos?

Pwedoh vair la leesta day vee-noss?
Could I see the wine list?

¿Qué me aconseja?

Kay may a-consay-ha?
What do you recommend?

Quiero una jarra de vino de la casa y una botella de agua mineral.

Key-airroh oona harra day vee-noh day la ca-sa ee oona bott-ay-ya day agwa minairral.
I would like a carafe of house wine and a bottle of mineral water.

¿Qué tiene sin alcohol?

Kay tee-enay sin alcoh-ol?
What soft drinks have you got?

Lo siento mucho, se me ha volcado el vaso.

Lo see-entoh moochoh, say may ah volcah-doh el vahsoh.
I'm sorry, I've spilt my drink.

Tenemos un poco de prisa.

Tenaymoss oon pohcoh day preesa.
We are in a bit of a hurry.

Problems with the bill

Perdone. ¿Qué quiere decir esto?

Peardonay. Kay kee-airray deth-earr estoh?
Excuse me. What does this mean?

91

The Menu

Churros
Chew-rross
Fritters

Jamón
Ham-on
Ham

Tostadas
Toss-tardass
Toast

Queso
Kayzoh
Cheese

Mantequilla y confitura
Mantay-keeya ee
confeetourra
Butter and jam

Paella
Pie-ay-ya
Rice dish

Bocadillo
Bockadee-yo
Sandwich

Chorizo
Choh-rreethoh
Spicy sausage

Ensalada
Ensa-ladda
Salad

Tortilla
Torr-teeya
Omelette

Restaurant Menu

Keep a look out for restaurants which have a special set menu, called a
Plato Combinado, Menú Turístico or a *Menú del Día*. This is cheaper
than choosing from the ordinary menu. *Vino Incluido* means that wine
is included in the price.

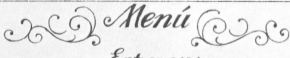

Menú

Entremeses
Starters

Chacinas
Chatheenass
Pork meats

Mariscos
Mareesscoss
Shellfish

Aceitunas
A-thay-too-nass
Olives

Gambas
Gambass
Prawns

Mejillones
Meh-he-yoness
Mussels

Cigalas
Thee-galess
Crayfish

Ostras
Ostrass
Oysters

Sopa
Soup

Gazpacho
Gathpatchoh
Chilled salad soup

Sopa de ajo
Sohpa day a-hoh
Garlic soup

Patatas fritas
Pa-ta-tass freetass
Chips

Café solo
Cafay solo
Black coffee

Helado
Ell-addoh
Ice cream

Café con leche
Cafay con lechay
White coffee

Pasteles
Pastelless
Cakes

Té con leche
Tay con lechay
Tea with milk

Pinchitos
Pincheetoss
Kebabs

Chocolate caliente
Chocolahtay
calee-entay
Hot chocolate

Hamburguesa
Amburrguessa
Hamburger

Zumo de naranja
Thoomoh day
na-ranha
Orange juice

Carne
Meat

Verduras y legumbres

Cochinillo asado
Cochineeyo a-sahdoh
Roast suckling pig

Cocido
Cotheedoh
Meat and bean casserole

Vegetables

Pescado
Fish

Lenguado
Len-gwadoh
Sole

Trucha
Troocha
Trout

Zarzuela
Tharrthooayla
Spicy fish stew

Postre
Last course

Fruta
Froota
Fruit

Tarta de Manzana
Tarta day manthana
Apple tart

Queso
Kayzoh
Cheese

Entertainments 1

To find out what is on in the area, look in a local paper, or ask at the nearest tourist office (*Oficina de Turismo*). If you are staying in a hotel, the receptionist may be able to help. When you go to the cinema or the theatre, you are expected to tip the usherette.

¿Hay algún espectáculo bueno?

Eye algoon espectak-ooloh booenoh?
Can you recommend a show to see?

Circo
Theerco
Circus

Teatro de Marionetas
Tayatroh day Marryon-etass
Puppet Theatre

Una Película de Dibujos Animados
Oona Peleek-oola day Deeboohoss Aneemahdoss
Cartoon Film

Teatro al Aire Libre
Tayatroh al Eye-ray Leebray
Open-Air Theatre

Un Parque de Atracciones
Oon Parkay day At-track-theeoness
A Fairground

Una Pantomima
Oona Pantomeema
A Pantomime

Luz y Sonido
Looth ee Soneedoh
Sound and Light Show
(These tell the story of famous old buildings in which they are held.)

Un Prestidigitador
Oon Presteedee-hitahdoor
A Magician

Un Partido de Fútbol
Oon Parteedoh day Footboll
A Football Match

¿Qué ponen esta noche en el cine?

Kay pon-en esta nochay en el theenay?
What is on at the cinema tonight?

¿Hay una película en inglés?

Eye oona peleek-oola en ingless?
Is there a film in English?

¿Cuánto es?

Cwantoe ess?
How much are the tickets?

Dos butacas

Doss bootackass
Two seats in the stalls.

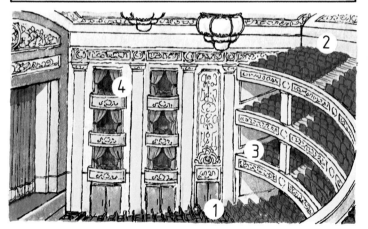

1 El Patio de Butacas
El Pateeoh day Bootackass
The Stalls

2 El Gallinero
El Gah-yeenairro
The Gallery

3 El Anfiteatro
El Anfee-tayatroh
The Dress Circle

4 Los Palcos
Loss Palcoss
Boxes

Entertainments 2

¿A qué hora empieza el espectáculo?

A las seis y media. Termina a las ocho.

Ah kay orra empee-etha el espectak-ooloh?
What time does the show begin?

Ah lass say-eess ee meddy-a. Tear-meena ah lass och-oh.
At six-thirty p.m. It finishes at eight p.m.

¿Dónde puedo comprar un programa?

La acomodadora los vende.

Donday pwedoh comprarr oon program-a?
Where can I buy a programme?

La acomoddadorr-a loss venday.
The usherette sells them.

Theatre signs

EL GUARDARROPA

Cloakroom

Salida de Emergencia

Fire exit

SERVICIOS

Toilets

PROHIBIDO FUMAR

No smoking

ÚNICAMENTE MAYORES 18 AÑOS

This sign means that children under the age of 18 are not allowed to see the show.

96

Sightseeing 1

The *Oficina de Turismo* will also give you sightseeing information. You will sometimes have to pay an entrance fee to visit places of interest. Museums are often closed, for all or half the day, on Mondays. A few places are closed during the winter.

¿Qué hay de interés en la ciudad?

Kay eye day interress en la thew-dath?
What is there of interest to see in the town?

Places to go sightseeing

El Castillo
El Casteeyo
The Castle

El Jardín Zoológico
El Hardine Thoo-oloh-heeko
The Zoo

El Museo
El Moosayoh
The Museum

La Iglesia
La Iglesseeya
The Church

El Barrio Antiguo
El Barryo Anteegwo
Old Part of Town

Parque Nacional
Parkay Natheeonarl
National Park

Las Cuevas
Lass Cwevass
Caves

¿Hay un mapa turístico de la ciudad?

Eye oon ma- pa too-reesteeko day la thew-dath?
Is there a tourist map of the town?

¿Puede decirme cuándo está abierto el museo?

Pweday dethearrmay cwandoe esta abby-airtoh el moosayoh?
Can you tell me when the museum is open?

Todos las días, excepto los lunes, desde las 9 hasta la 1.

Todoss loss dee-ass, ectheptoh loss looness, desday lass noo-evay hasta la oona.
Every day, except Monday, from 9 a.m. to 1 p.m.

¿Cuánto es la entrada?

Cwantoe ess la entrahda?
How much is the admission charge?

Sightseeing 2

Guided tours

¿Hay una visita con guía en inglés?

Eye oona veeseeta con geea en ingless?
Is there a guided tour in English?

Sí. La próxima visita empieza dentro de un cuarto de hora.

See. La proxeema veeseeta empee-etha dentro day oon cwarto day orra.
Yes the next tour starts in a quarter of an hour.

¿Cuánto dura la visita?

Cwantoe doora la veeseeta?
How long does the tour last?

¿Se puede subir a la torre?

Say pweday soo-beer ah la torray?
Can one go up the tower?

At the zoo

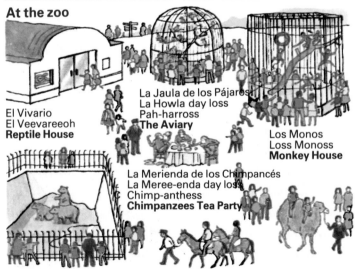

El Vivario
El Veevareeoh
Reptile House

La Jaula de los Pájaros
La Howla day loss Pah-harross
The Aviary

Los Monos
Loss Monoss
Monkey House

La Merienda de los Chimpancés
La Meree-enda day loss Chimp-anthess
Chimpanzees Tea Party

El Foso de los Osos
El Fossoh day loss Ossoss
Bear Pit

Paseos en Burro
Passayos en Boorroh
Donkey rides

Paseos en Camello
Passayos en Cam-ay-yo
Camel rides

Signs

Do not feed the Animals

Dangerous Animals

Wild Animals

Entrance

Exit

Do not Touch

Cameras Prohibited

Tea-Room

Private Property

Beware of the Dog

No Entrance

Closed for the Holidays

Open

Closed

Keep off the Grass

Making Friends

Hola. ¿Cómo te llamas?

Me llamo María. ¿Y tú?

Oh-la. Com-o tay yamass?
Hello. What is your name?

May ya-mo Ma-rreea. Ee too?
My name is Maria. And yours?

¿Dónde vives?

Vivo allí.

Donday veevess?
Where are you staying?

Veevoh eye-ee.
I live over there.

¿Cuántos años tienes?

Tengo doce años.

Cwantoss an-yoss tee-eness?
How old are you?

Tengo dothay an-yoss.
I'm 12.

Éste es mi hermano Juan. ¿Tienes hermanos o hermanas?

Estay ess mee airrmanoh Hooan. Tee-eness airrmanoss oh airrman-ass?
This is my brother Juan. Have you any brothers or sisters?

Sí. Tengo una hermana mayor. Y éste es mi hermano gemelo.

See. Tengo oona airrmana my- orr. Ee estay ess me airrmanoh hem-ello.
Yes. I have an elder sister. And here is my twin brother.

¿Puedes comer con nosotros?

Pwedess comair con noss-otross?
Can you have lunch with us?

Tengo que preguntar a mis padres.

Tengo kay praygoontarr ah mees pah-dress.
I must ask my parents.

¡Vamos a jugar!

Va-moss ah hoo-garr.
Let's go and play.

¡Date prisa!   ¡Espérame!

¡Ya voy!

Dahtay preesa!
Hurry up!

Ya voy!
I'm coming!

Espearra-may!
Wait for me!

Me gusta . . .

May goosta . . .
I like . . .

El ajedrez
El a-headrreth
Chess

Pintar
Pintarr
Painting

La Filatelia
La Feelatell-eea
Stamp Collecting

Cards

Oros
Oh-ross
Diamonds

Copas
Coh-pass
Hearts

Bastos
Basstoss
Clubs

Espadas
Espah-dass
Spades

El Rey
El Ray
King

La Reina
La Rayeena
Queen

La Sota
La Sohta
Jack

El As
El Ass
Ace

El Comodín
El Coh-moh-deen
Joker

Playing Games

¡Ve a buscarlo!
Vay ah booscarrloh!
Go and get it!

¡Te toca a ti!
Tay tocka ah tee!
It's your turn!

Juego del escondite
Hooay-goh del escondeetay
Hide and Seek

Montar en bicicleta
Montarr en beetheekleta
Bicycling

¡Tírame el balón!
Tier-ramay el bal-on!
Throw me the ball!

¡Cógelo!
Coh-hayloh!
Catch!

A la Pata Ciega
Ah la Pa-ta Theeayga
Hopscotch

El Columpio
El Col-umpee-oh
Swing

Se llama la Pelota.

Say ya-ma la Pelotta
It's called Pelota.

¿A qué estáis jugando?

Ah kay es-tie-ees hoogandoh?
What are you playing?

Jugar a saltar la burra
Hoogarr ah saltarr la boorra
Leap Frog

¿Quién gana?

Key-en gana?
Who is winning?

A las Tabas
Ah lass Tabass
Jacks

A las Canicas
Ah lass Canee-cass
Marbles

103

Sports

There is a lot of good fishing in Spain, especially for salmon, trout, pike and carp. For fishing in lakes and rivers, you need a permit from the *Delegación de Turismo* in the province concerned. This will cost about 500 pesetas.

Going fishing

¿Dónde puedo alquilar una caña de pescar?

Donday pwedoh alkee-lar oona can-ya day pess-carr?
Where can I hire a fishing rod?

¿Cuánto es por día?

Cwantoe ess pour deea?
How much does it cost for the day?

¿Necesito un permiso?

Nethess-eetoh oon pear-meesoh?
Must one have a permit?

Perdone. ¿Tiene usted cebo para pescar?

Peardonay. Tee-enay oo-sted thay-boh pa-ra pess-carr?
Have you any bait, please?

¿Es un buen sitio para pescar?

Ess oon booen seatee-oh pa-ra pess-carr?
Is this a good place to fish?

Riding

¿Se puede montar a caballo por aquí?

Say pweyday montarr ah cab-eye-yo pour a-key?
Can one go riding near here?

Querríamos unas lecciones de equitación.

Kair-ree-amoss oonass lecthee-ownays day eh-keytatheeon.
We would like some riding lessons.

104

Skiing

Las Botas de Esquiar
Lass bohtass day ess-key-arr
Ski Boots

Los Esquís
Loss ess-keys
Skis

Los Bastones de Esquiar
Loss bass-toness day ess-key-arr
Ski Sticks

Los Guantes
Loss gwantess
Ski Gloves

Un Abono
Oon a-bon-oh
Ski Pass

¿Dónde está la escuela de esquí

Donday esta la es-cwela day ess-key?
Where is the ski school?

The ski runs

The ski runs, or Pistas, are marked with coloured arrows.

Nursery slopes— very easy.

Beginners—easy.

For quite experienced skiers—quite difficult.

For professional skiers— very difficult.

Soy un principiante

Soy oon printhee-pee-antay.
I am a beginner.

Yo ya he esquiado una vez

Yoh ya ay ess-key-addoh oona veth.
I have skied once before.

Sé esquiar bien.

Say ess-key-arr beeyen.
I can ski well.

No puedo levantarme. ¿Puede ayudarme?

No pwedoh lev-antarr-may. Pweday ay-oodarr-may?
I cannot get up. Can you help me?

Nos hemos perdido. ¿Dónde está el telesquí?

Noss ay-moss peardeedoh. Donday esta el telesskey?
We are lost. Where is the ski-lift?

At the Seaside 1

¿Dónde está la playa más cercana?

¿Hay una piscina?

Donday esta la ply-a mass thair-cana?
Where is the nearest beach?

Eye oona peas-theena?
Is there a swimming pool?

Quiero alquilar dos colchonetas, una hamaca . . .

. . . y una sombrilla

Key-airroh alkee-lar doss colchon-etass, oona amaca . . .
I would like to hire two mattresses, a deck chair . . .

. . . ee oona sombree-ya.
. . . and a parasol.

¿Dónde puedo cambiarme?

Al lado de la piscina para niños.

¿Donday pwedoh cambee-arrmay?
Where are the changing rooms?
Al lahdoh day la peas-theena pa-ra neen-yoss.
Next to the paddling pool.

Beach things

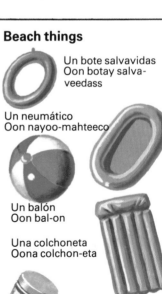

Un bote salvavidas
Oon botay salva-veedass

Un neumático
Oon nayoo-mahteeco

Un balón
Oon bal-on

Una colchoneta
Oona colchon-eta

Crema para el sol
Krayma pa-ra el sol

Hola. ¿Vamos a nadar?

Oh-la. Va-moss ah nahdarr?
Hello. Let's go for a swim.

Por favor, ¿puede cuidarme mis cosas?

Pour favorr, pweday cwee-darrmay mees coss-ass?
Please could you look after my things for me?

¡Cuidado! ¡Viene una ola grande!

Cweedahdoh! Vee-enay oona olla granday!
Watch out! There's a big wave coming!

¿Hay una ducha?

Eye oona doo-cha?
Is there a shower?

Páseme la toalla.

Pahsaymay la toh-eye-ya.
Pass me the towel.

El Esquí Náutico
El Eskey Nahooteecoh
Water Skiing

Pedalo
Peh-dah-loh
Pedalo

Un Barco de Vela
Oon Barr-coh day Vayla
Sailing boat

107

At the Seaside 2

¿Hacemos un castillo de arena?

¿Tienes un pozal y una pala?

A-thaymoss oon casteeyo day ah-rayna?
Shall we build a sand castle?
Tee-eness oon poth-al ee oona pahla?
Have you got a bucket and spade?

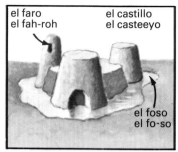

el faro
el fah-roh

el castillo
el casteeyo

el foso
el fo-so

¿Qué significa la bandera roja?

Kay signeefeeka la bandairra roha?
What does the red flag mean?

Es peligroso nadar.
El mar está agitado.

PROHIBIDO BAÑARSE

Ess pelee-grosso nahdarr. El marr esta a-hee-tahdoh.
It is dangerous to swim. The sea is too rough.

No Bathing

Tengo calor.

Tengo cal-orr.
I'm hot.

Vamos a comprar un helado.

Va-moss ah comprarr oon elladdoh.
Let's go and buy an ice cream.

Buying an ice cream

HELADOS

Perdone, ¿tiene helados?

Peardonay, tee-enay ell-addoss?
Excuse me, do you have any ice creams.

Sí. ¿De qué sabor?

See. Day kay sa-borr?
Yes. What flavour would you like?

Vainilla
Vy-neeya
Vanilla

Fresa
Fressa
Strawberry

Frambuesa
Fram-boo-essa
Raspberry

Nueces
Noo-ethess
Nutty

Pistacho
Pea-stahcho
Pistachio

Chocolate
Chocolahtay
Chocolate

Quiero un helado de vainilla.

Key-airroh oon elladdoh day vy-neeya.
I would like a vanilla ice cream.

¿Normal o doble?

Norr-mall oh doblay?
A single or a double?

Un polo grande de fresa.

Oon pol-oh granday day fressa.
A large strawberry lolly.

¿Cuánto es?

Cwantoe ess?
How much is it?

Treinta pesetas.

Tray-inta pessay-tass.
Thirty pesetas.

Gracias.

Grathee-ass.
Thank you.

109

Accidents and Emergencies

You can find the numbers for fire, police and ambulance services on the wall inside a public telephone box. Road accidents should be reported to the police station (*Comisaría*). If you are in serious trouble, contact a British Consulate.

¡Socorro!

Soh-coh-rroh!
Help!

¡Vengan pronto!

Veng-gann pronto!
Come quickly!

¡Fuego!

Foo-eggoh!
Fire!

Por favor, llamen una ambulancia.

Pour favorr, ya-men oona amboolantheea.
Please call for an ambulance.

Missing persons

Mi amigo falta desde anoche.

Me ameegoh fal-ta desday a-nochay.
My friend has been missing since last night.

¿Cúando lo vio por última vez?

¿Cwandoe lo veeoh pour oolteema veth?
Where did you last see him?

Llevaba una bufanda y un sombrero rojos.

Yev-ah-ba oona boofanda ee oon sombrairroh roh-hoss.
He was wearing a red hat and scarf.

Salió a las seis a comprar un periódico.

Sallyo a lass sayeess a comprarr oon perryoddy-coe.
He went out at 6.00 p.m. to buy a newspaper.

Lost or stolen

He perdido mi pasaporte.

Ay peardeedoh me passa- portay.
I have lost my passport.

Me han robado el billetero

May an robaddoh el beeyetairro.
My wallet has been stolen.

Other things

mis cheques
de viaje
mees checkess
day veeah-hay
**my
traveller's
cheques**

mi cámera
fotográfica
me ca-maira
foto-grafee-
cah
my camera

mi maleta
me malet-a
my suitcase

mis llaves
mees ya-vess
my keys

mi bolso
me bolsoh
my bag

mi reloj
me rel-ohh
my watch

Han entrado a robar en mi habitación.

An entrahdoh ah rohbarr en me abeetatheeon.
My room has been burgled.

Pasó entre las dos de la noche y mediodía.

Passoh entray lass doss day la nochay ee meddy-oh-deea.
It happened between 10.00 p.m. and midday.

¿Dónde podemos ponernos en contacto con usted?

Donday podaymoss ponairnoss en contactoh con oo-sted.
Where can we contact you.

Aquí tiene mi nombre y dirección.

A-key tee-enay me nombray ee dee-recktheeon.
Here is my name and address.

Using the Telephone

In Spain you can find public telephones in many cafés and shops, or you could look for a telephone box, or *cabina telefónica*. The telephone system works independently of the post office, so you will not find telephones there. If you want to make long distance calls, or look up numbers in the directories, you could go to the telephone exchange, or *central telefónica*.

Most telephones are coin-operated. You can use either 5, 25, or 50 peseta pieces. Before dialling, you line up the coin or coins in a rack above the dial. When you have dialled the number, you should hear a series of rapid pips. This is the ringing tone. When the call is answered, one of the coins will fall into a slot. When the time runs out, another coin will fall in.

Many telephone boxes are for local calls only. To call another town or country, look for a box with a green strip across the top, marked *"interurbano"*.

PRESS THIS BUTTON TO CALL THE OPERATOR

YOU PUT THE COINS HERE

Perdone, ¿puedo usar su teléfono?

Peardonay, pwedoh oosarr soo tel-efonoh?
Please may I use the telephone?

Making a phone call

Quiero poner una conferencia para Londres, a cobro revertido. El número es 800 6009.

Key-airroh pon-airr oonah confair-entheea pa-ra Londress ah cob-rroh reh-vairteedoh. El noomairroh ess 800 6009.
I want to call London and reverse the charges. The number is London 800 6009.

Por favor, ¿puede darme cambio?

Pour favorr, pweday darrmay cambee-oh?
Please could you give me some change?

¿Cuál es su número?
No cuelgue.

Cwal ess soo noomairroh?
No cwel-gay.
What is your number? Hold the line.

Se ha equivocado de número.

Say ah eh-keyvoc-addoh day noomairroh. **Wrong number**.

¿Puedo hablar con el señor Pérez, por favor?

¿Pwedoh ab-lar con el sen-yorr Perreth, pour favorr?
Please may I speak to Mr Perez?

Está comunicando.

Esta commooneecando.
The number is engaged.

No está aquí en este momento.

¿Quién habla?

No esta a-key en estay mo-mentoh.
He is not here at the moment.

Key-en ab-la?
Who is speaking?

Por favor, podría decirle que la señora Brown llamó por teléfono, y perdirle que llame a este número.

Pour favorr, podreea deth-ear lay kay la sen-yorra Brown ya-mo pour tel-efonoh ee pear-dearrlay kay ya-may ah estay noomairroh.
Could you tell him that Mrs Brown telephoned, and ask him to ring me at this number.

Feeling ill

The *farmacia* will be able to give you advice and medicines for most minor ailments. If you see a doctor you will have to pay him on the spot. There is no free medical treatment in Spain. In case of an emergency, ask for a *médico de urgencia*.

Tengo dolor de cabeza.
Tengo dolorr day cabetha.
I have a headache.

Tengo dolor de estómago.
Tengo dolorr day estoma-go.
I have a stomach pain.

Tengo un resfriado.
Tengo oon resfree-addoh.
I have a cold.

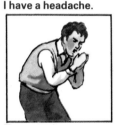

Toso mucho.
Tossoh moochoh.
I am coughing a lot.

Tengo fiebre.
Tengo fee-ebbray.
I have a temperature.

Tengo ganas de vomitar.
Tengo ganass day vomee-tarr.
I feel sick.

Me he cortado.
May ay corr-tah-doh.
I have cut myself.

Me he quemado.
May ay kay-mah-doh.
I have burnt myself.

Tengo una insolación.
Tengo oona insoh-lah-theeon.
I am suffering from sunstroke.

Me ha picado (mordido) . . .
May ah pee-cah-doh (more-deedo) . . .
I have been stung or bitten by . . .

una medusa.
oona medoosa.
a jellyfish.

un erizo de mar
oon eh-reethoh day marr.
a sea-urchin.

una serpiente.
oona sairpee-entay.
a snake.

una avispa.
oona avees-pa.
a wasp.

114

Tengo algo en el ojo.
Tengo algo en el oh-hoe.
I have something in my eye.

Tengo una erupción.
Tengo oona eh-roop-theeon.
I have a rash.

Me pica.
May pee-ca.
It itches.

Tengo dolor de muelas.
Tengo dolorr day moo-elass.
I have toothache.

Me ha atacado un perro.
May ah ah-tackahdoh oon pearroh.
I have been attacked by a dog.

Me he roto la pierna.
May ay roh-toh la pee-airr-na.
I have broken my leg.

Going to the doctor

Necesito ver un médico.

Nethesseetoh vair oon mehdeecoh.
I need to see a doctor.

¿Cuándo está libre?

Cwandoe esta leebray?
When is he free?

¿Me puede vacunar contra el tétano?

May pweday vah-coonarr contra el tet-ah-noh?
Can you innoculate me against tetanus?

¿Puede recetarme algo?

Pweday rehthettarr-may algo?
Can you give me a prescription?

Parts of the Body

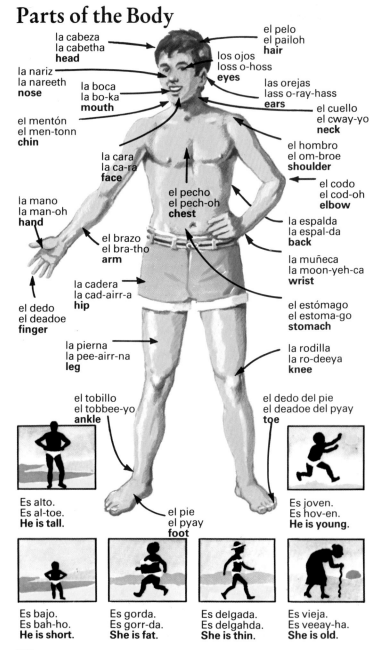

la cabeza
la cabetha
head

el pelo
el pailoh
hair

los ojos
loss o-hoss
eyes

la nariz
la nareeth
nose

las orejas
lass o-ray-hass
ears

la boca
la bo-ka
mouth

el cuello
el cway-yo
neck

el mentón
el men-tonn
chin

la cara
la ca-ra
face

el hombro
el om-broe
shoulder

el codo
el cod-oh
elbow

el pecho
el pech-oh
chest

la mano
la man-oh
hand

la espalda
la espal-da
back

el brazo
el bra-tho
arm

la muñeca
la moon-yeh-ca
wrist

la cadera
la cad-airr-a
hip

el estómago
el estoma-go
stomach

el dedo
el deadoe
finger

la pierna
la pee-airr-na
leg

la rodilla
la ro-deeya
knee

el tobillo
el tobbee-yo
ankle

el dedo del pie
el deadoe del pyay
toe

el pie
el pyay
foot

Es alto.
Es al-toe.
He is tall.

Es joven.
Es hov-en.
He is young.

Es bajo.
Es bah-ho.
He is short.

Es gorda.
Es gorr-da.
She is fat.

Es delgada.
Es delgahda.
She is thin.

Es vieja.
Es veeay-ha.
She is old.

Colours
Colores (Col-orress)

negro
neg-roe
black

blanco
blang-coe
white

gris
grease
grey

color arena
collaw a-rain-a
beige

marrón
ma-rron
brown

amarillo
amma-reeyo
yellow

naranja
na-ranha
orange

rojo
roh-ho
red

rosa
ross-a
pink

violeta
veeol-etta
violet

azul
a-thool
blue

verde
vairrday
green

oro
orow
gold

plata
platta
silver

oscuro
os-cure-o
dark

claro
cla-roe
light

Months, Seasons and Days

Enero
En-airroh
January

Febrero
Febrair-roe
February

Marzo
Marr-thoe
March

Abril
Ab-reel
April

Mayo
My-yo
May

Junio
Hoon-y-oh
June

Julio
Hool-y-oh
July

Agosto
A-goss-toe
August

Septiembre
Septee-embray
September

Octubre
Octoobray
October

Noviembre
Novee-embray
November

Diciembre
Deethee-embray
December

La Semana (La Sem-ahna)

7 Lunes
Looness
Monday

8 Martes
Marrtess
Tuesday

9 Miércoles
Me-airr-coless
Wednesday

10 Jueves
Hoo-evess
Thursday

11 Viernes
Vee-airness
Friday

12 Sábado
Sabaddoh
Saturday

13 Domingo
Doming-goh
Sunday

La Primavera
La Preemavair-ra
The Spring

El Verano
El Vair-anno
The Summer

El Otoño
El O-tonn-yo
The Autumn

El Invierno
El Invee-airrno
The Winter

119

The Weather

El Tiempo
Ell Tea-empoh

Llueve.
You-evay.
It's raining.

Va a llover.
Va ah yov-airr.
It's going to rain.

Graniza.
Gran-eetha.
It's hailing.

Hace viento.
A-thay vee-entoh.
It's windy.

Nieva.
Knee-eva.
It's snowing.

Está nublado.
Esta noo-bladoh.
It's cloudy.

Truena.
True-ayna.
It's thundering.

Un relámpago.
Oon rel-am-pagoh.
A flash of lightening.

Hace fresco.
A-thay frescoh.
It's cool.

Hace bueno.
A-thay booenoh.
It's a nice day.

Hace calor.
A-thay calorr.
It's hot.

Hace frío.
A-thay free-oh.
It's cold.

Numbers

1 Uno Oon-oh	16 Dieciséis Dee-ethee-sayeess	40 Cuarenta Cwa-renta
2 Dos Doss	17 Diecisiete Dee-ethee-see-etay	50 Cincuenta Thing-cwenta
3 Tres Tress	18 Dieciocho Dee-ethee-och-oh	60 Sesenta Sess-enta
4 Cuatro Cwatroe	19 Diecinueve Dee-ethee-noo-evay	70 Setenta Set-enta
5 Cinco Thing-co	20 Veinte Vay-intay	80 Ochenta Och-enta
6 Seis Say-eess	21 Veintiuno Vay-intee-oonoh	90 Noventa Nov-enta
7 Siete See-etay	22 Veintidós Vay-intee-doss	100 Cien Thee-en
8 Ocho Och-oh	23 Veintitrés Vay-intee-tress	101 Ciento uno Thee-entoh oonoh
9 Nueve Noo-evay	24 Veinticuatro Vay-intee-cwatroe	200 Doscientos (as) * Doss-thee-entoss (ass)*
10 Diez Dee-eth	25 Veinticinco Vay-intee-thingco	1,000 Mil Meal
11 Once Onthay	26 Veintiséis Vay-intee-say-eess	1,001 Mil uno Meal oonoh
12 Doce Dothay	27 Veintisiete Vay-intee-see-etay	2,000 Dos mil Doss meal
13 Trece Trethay	28 Veintiocho Vay-intee-och-oh	1,000,000 Un millón Oon meal-yon
14 Catorce Catorrthay	29 Veintinueve Vay-intee-noo-evay	1st Primero (a)* Premairroh (a) *
15 Quince Kinthay	30 Treinta Tray-inta	2nd Segundo (a)* Segoondo (a) *

*This shows the ending to use with a feminine word.

The Time

In Spain the 24 hour clock is used, so times after midday are written as 1300, 1400 and so on. Another point to remember is that the Spanish say, for example, "it is nine minus ten", instead of "ten minutes to nine", as we do.

¿Qué hora es, por favor?

Kay orra ess, pour favorr?
What time is it please?

Son las ocho.
Sonn lass och-oh.
It is eight o'clock.

Son las ocho y cuarto.
Sonn lass och-oh ee cwarto.
It is quarter past eight.

Son las nueve menos cuarto.
Sonn lass noo-evay menoss cwarto.
It is quarter to nine.

Es el mediodía.
Ess el meddy-oh-deea.
It is midday.

Son las cinco menos cinco.
Sonn lass thing-co menoss thing-co.
It is five to five.

Son las siete y diez.
Sonn lass see-etay ee dee-eth.
It is ten past seven.

Son las diez y media.
Sonn lass dee-eth ee meddy-a.
It is half past ten.

Es la medianoche.
Ess la meddy-a-nochay.
It is midnight.

la mañana
la man-yan-a
the morning

la tarde
la tarrday
**the afternoon and
the evening**

la noche
la nochay
the night

Time phrases

ayer ah-yair **yesterday**	este año es-tay an-yo **this year**	temprano temprahnoe **early**	dentro de cinco minutos dentro day thing-co minootoss **in five minutes**
hoy oi **today**	el mes pasado el mess pas- addoh **last month**	más temprano mass temprahnoe **earlier**	
mañana man-yan-a **tomorrow**	la semana que viene la sem-ahna kay vee-enay **next week**	pronto pronto **soon**	dentro de un cuarto de hora dentro day oon cwarto day orra **in a quarter of an hour**
anteayer antay-ah-yair **the day before yesterday**	ahora a-orra **now**	más tarde mass tarrday **later**	dentro de media hora dentro day meddy-a orra **in half an hour**
pasado mañana pas-addo man-yan-a **the day after tomorrow**		nunca noonka **never**	dentro de una hora dentro day oona orra **in an hour**

Basic Grammar
Nouns

All Spanish nouns are either masculine or feminine. When you learn a noun, you must learn this as well. Many nouns end with an "o", and these are nearly always masculine. Nouns ending with an "a" are usually feminine. The word for "the" is *el* before masculine (m) nouns and *la* before feminine (f) nouns.

e.g. *el libro* (the book)
la casa (the house)

If the noun is plural (p), the word for "the" is *los* before masculine nouns and *las* before feminine nouns.

e.g. *los libros* (the books)
las casas (the houses)

Spanish nouns ending with a vowel have an "*s*" in the plural. Nouns ending with a consonant have "*es*".
e.g. *la flor* (the flower)
las flores (the flowers)
la casa (the house)
las casas (the houses)

The Spanish for "a" or "an" is *un* before a masculine noun and *una* before a feminine noun.

e.g. *un libro* (a book)
una casa (a house)

Pronouns

The Spanish word for "it" or "they" depends on whether the noun it replaces is masculine or feminine.

e.g. *el gato come* (the cat eats)
él come (it eats)

In Spanish the verb can be used on its own, without the subject pronouns. Subject pronouns are used to create emphasis.

I	*yo*
you	*tú*
he, it (m)	*él*
she, if (f)	*ella*
you (polite form)	*usted*
we	*nosotros*
you (p)	*vosotros*
they (m)	*ellos*
they (f)	*ellas*
you (p) (polite form)	*ustedes*

Possessive adjectives

The word you use for "my", "your", "his" etc. depends on whether the word that follows it is masculine, feminine or plural.

e.g. *nuestro libro* (m) (our book)
nuestra casa (f) (our house)
nuestros libros (m) (pl) (our books)

	Singular		Plural	
	(m)	**(f)**	**(m)**	**(f)**
my	mi	mi	mis	mis
your	tu	tu	tus	tus
his, her, its your (polite form)	su	su	sus	sus
our	nuestro	nuestra	nuestros	nuestras
your (p)	vuestro	vuestra	vuestros	vuestras
their, your (p) (polite form)	su	su	sus	sus

Useful verbs

There are two verbs meaning "to be" in Spanish: *ser* and *estar*. *Ser* is used to describe people and things and for telling the time. *Estar* is used to describe the position of things, such as "He is in America." and temporary conditions, such as, "It is raining."

ser	to be
yo soy	I am
tú eres	you are
él es	he is
ella es	she is
usted es	you are (polite form)
nosotros somos	we are
vosotros sois	you are (p)
ellos son	they are (m)
ellas son	they are (f)
ustedes son	you are (p) (polite form)

estar	to be
yo estoy	I am
tú estás	you are
él está	he is
ella está	she is
usted está	you are (polite form)
nosotros estamos	we are
vosotros estáis	you are (p)
ellos están	they are (m)
ellas están	they are (f)
ustedes están	you are (pl) (polite form)

tener	to have
tengo	I have
tienes	you have
tiene	he, she, it has you have (polite form)
tenemos	we have
tenéis	you have (p)
tienen	they have you have (p) (polite form)

hablar	to speak
hablo	I speak
hablas	you speak
habla	he, she, it speaks you speak (polite form)
hablamos	we speak
habláis	you speak (p)
hablan	they speak you speak (p) (polite form)

ir	to go
voy	I go
vas	you go
va	he, she, it goes you go (polite form)
vamos	we go
vais	you go (p)
van	they go you go (p) (polite form)

vivir	to live
vivo	I live
vives	you live
vive	he, she, it lives you live (polite form)
vivimos	we live
vivís	you live (p)
viven	they live you live (p) (polite form)

Negatives

To make a verb negative, add *no* before the verb.

e.g. *Hablo español*
  I speak Spanish
  No hablo español
  I do not speak Spanish

Questions . . .

There are two ways you can ask a question in Spanish. You can use your voice to make a statement sound like a question, or you can use the pronoun and put it after the verb.

e.g. *Quieres* You want
  ¿Quieres? Do you want?
  ¿Quieres tú? Do you want?

Index

This index lists some words individually and some under group names, such as food. Where you will find the Spanish for the indexed word, the page number is printed in italics, like this: *6*

Index of Spanish words

This index list some of the Spanish words you might see on signs and notices. Look up the page references to find out what they mean.